D1467720

NIAGARA FALLS

A PICTORIAL JOURNEY

"The Great Horseshoe – Niagara." Paul Thomas Hanover, 1991

Niagara Falls

A Pictorial Journey

Margaret Dunn

Photography by

Michael D. Romanowich

$\mathcal{A}cknowledgements$

Copyright 1998 Margaret Dunn
All rights reserved. No part of this publication may be reproduced, stored, or introduced into a retrieval system, or transmitted in any form by any means, electronic or mechanical, including photocopying, recording, or otherwise, without the prior written permission of the publisher and copyright owner, except for brief passages quoted by a reviewer.

Published in Niagara Falls, Canada, by Margaret Dunn
Address inquiries to:
Margaret Dunn, 7366 Edenwood Court, Niagara Falls, Ontario L2J 4E3
Tel: (905) 358-6348

Book Design: Campbell Creative Services, St. Catharines, Ontario
Color separations: Rainbow Digicolor Inc., Toronto, Ontario
Printed in Hong Kong by Book Art Inc., Toronto, Ontario

Canadian Cataloguing in Publication Data
Dunn, Margaret, 1950-
    Niagara Falls: a pictorial journey
Includes bibliographical references and index.
ISBN 0-9699126-1-7

1. Niagara Falls (N.Y. and Ont.) - Pictorial works. 2. Niagara Falls (N.Y. and Ont.) - History. I. Romanowich, Michael D. II. Title.

FC3095.N5D86 1998   971.3'39   C97-932245-6
FC127.N8D86 1998

The author gratefully acknowledges the enthusiasm, kindness and support of many who were instrumental to the production of this book. Special thanks to the following sponsors and contributors:

KODAK CANADA INC.

The color images in this book are evidence of the exceptional quality of Kodak film. We found Kodak Ektachrome 100 film unsurpassed in producing sharp, fine grained photos with excellent contrast. Special thanks to Brad Thompson.

RAINBOW AIR INC.

Photographing Niagara Falls entailed gaining access to unusual heights and angles. We relied on Rainbow Air of Niagara Falls, New York, a company with a reputation for high professional standards in flightseeing, aerial photography, air charter and long line helicopter cruises. Sincere thanks to Robert Culbreth, Matthew Sharpe and Philip Newson.

PAUL THOMAS HANOVER, ROLLING THUNDER ARTS, INC.

The Great Horseshoe – Niagara (preceding page) and Terrapin Tower – Niagara (page 31) are just two of the beautiful paintings by Paul Thomas Hanover in the collection, Landscape Into the Past and Present – Niagara. They have been published as limited edition prints by Paul Thomas Hanover, Rolling Thunder Arts, Inc., 1517 Main Street, Niagara Falls, New York, 14305 (Tel. 716-283-5338, 716-471-9798).

Acknowledgements

The author is grateful to **April Petrie** for the loan of the Francis Petrie Collection; to **Don Green** for the Fred Green Collection; to **Ruth Rosenberg** for the Len Rosenberg, Rochester Collection, and to **George Bailey**, **Robert Bracken**, **John Burtniak**, **Don Ede**, **Clarence Joyce**, **Ron Roels**, **Ron Schifferle** and **Sherman Zavitz** for sharing their own collections of Niagara Falls photos and memorabilia.

Thanks to **Pat Simon**, Simon's Restaurant, Niagara Falls, Ontario. Simon's is the oldest restaurant in the city and a meeting place for Niagara rivermen, Falls memorabilia collectors, and Niagara enthusiasts by vocation or pastime. Pat shared his own Niagara Falls collection and photographic equipment.

Sincere appreciation is extended to **George and Ruth Crawford** and **Janet Duval**, who proofread the manuscript, and to **Kathryn Docherty** for assistance with research and photo selection.

Thanks also to many others who provided invaluable support and assistance:

In New York State:
Eleanor Baran, Niagara Falls Area Chamber of Commerce
TSgt. Peter Borys, Niagara Falls Air Reserve Station
Steve Brady, Niagara Mohawk Power Corporation
Lee Brownschidle
Frank Clendening
Clyde Doty, New York State Park Police
Daniel Dumych, Local History Department, Niagara
    Falls Public Library

Melissa Dunlap, Niagara County Historical Society
Ava Ehde, Local History Department, Niagara Falls
    Public Library
Maureen Fennie, Local History Department, Niagara
    Falls Public Library
Doris Hampton, New York State Office of Parks,
    Recreation and Historic Preservation
Lou Harasty, Photographer
Thomas Loonan, Photography, Albright-Knox Art Gallery
Walter Mayer, Buffalo and Erie County Historical Society
Parke Morrow Jr., The Book Corner
Paul Pasquarello, New York Power Authority
Robert Salfi, New York Power Authority
Judie Takacs, Festival of Lights
Barry Virgilio, Schoellkopf Geological Museum
John White, Niagara Mohawk Power Corporation
Joanne Willmott, New York Power Authority

In Ontario:
Greg Bailey, Winter Festival of Lights
Len Cade, Best Western Cairn Croft
James Campbell, The Samuel E. Weir Collection &
    Library Of Art
Laurel Campbell, Harmony Prints Inc.
Walter Lord Charest, Canadian Niagara Power Co. Ltd.
Cathy Christopher, Oakes Inn
Jim Desson, Niagara River guide
Keith Fox, Aerial Photography Pilot (Cessna 180)
David Gillies, Skylon
Bob and Debbie Harasty
Laura MacFadden, Old Niagara Bookshop

Dan Martone, Ontario Hydro
Lori & David Mason
Tim Monroe
Linda Montreuil, Canadian Niagara Hotels Inc.
Roy Muir, Canadian Niagara Power Co. Ltd.
April and Melanie Mullen and family
Bob Osborne, Ontario Hydro
Andrew Porteus and reference staff, Niagara Falls
    Public Library
Rob and Dan Pozzobon, Ed and Stacey Pozzobon
Deborah Pratt, Inniskillin Winery
Nancy Quinn, Whirlpool Jet
Ann Marie Rondinelli, Marineland
Tim Ruddy, Maid of the Mist Steamboat Company, Ltd.
Jacob Sherman, Niagara Falls Museum
Ken Sloggett
Cindy Simon, Niagara Falls Business and Professional
    Women's Club
Frank Simon, Maid of the Mist Steamboat Company, Ltd.
Debbie Stark, Great Gorge Adventure, and Sam Stark
Peggy Steele, Imax Theatre and Daredevil Adventure
Margaret Anne Tabaka, Lundy's Lane Historical
    Museum
Cheryl Tyndall, Niagara Parks Butterfly Conservatory
Bert & Norm Watson, Double Deck Tours

Last but not least, thanks to my husband, Bill, and my children, Sarah, Scott, Patricia and Geordie, for their enthusiasm in sharing in this project about their birthplace, Niagara Falls, the world's most famous address.

This book is dedicated to my father, George Crawford. A civil engineer, he became President of Gore and Storrie Limited, Consulting Engineers, and an acknowledged expert in the water environment field. His lifelong interest in water has been as relentless as the mighty Niagara.

Contents

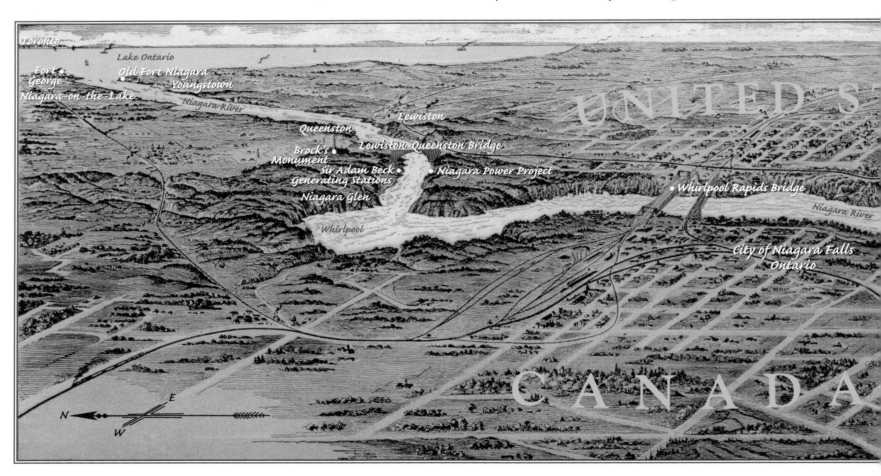

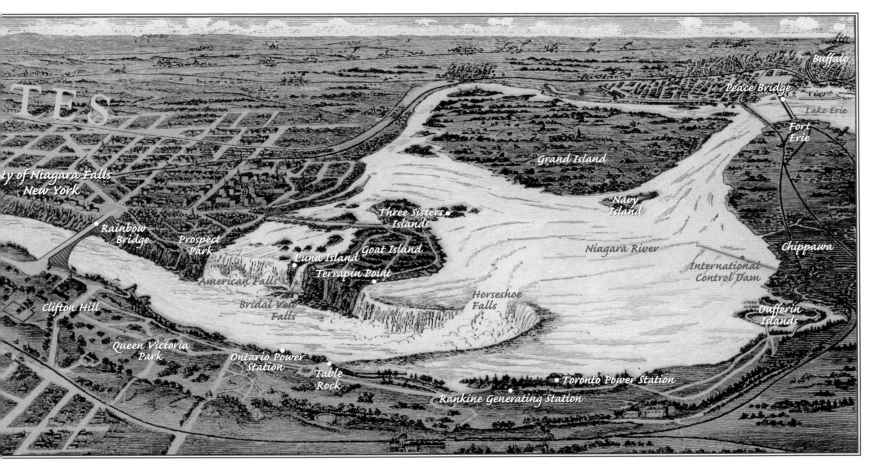

Based on an engraving in "The Falls of Niagara", published by Knight, Leonard & Co., Chicago, 1892
Adaptation by Rose Ellen Campbell, Campbell Creative Services

Sightseers come from all over the world to see Niagara Falls. Paintings and poems, photographs and internet websites celebrate its unique natural beauty and power. This mighty plunge in the Niagara River is world famous.

On its brief but riotous journey from Lake Erie to Lake Ontario, the Niagara River drops an astounding 99 meters (326 feet). About halfway along its course, the river forks and pours over giant waterfalls. The largest is the Horseshoe Falls, curving in a great arc from Goat Island, New York, to the Canadian shore. The American Falls and Bridal Veil Falls on the west bank complete this scene of wonderment that has inspired awe in millions of visitors.

The sheer volume of water pouring over the Falls is magnificent. The Niagara River has a total average flow of about 6000 cubic meters per second (212,000 cubic feet per second). Canada and the United States share some of the water flow for hydroelectric power generation. An international treaty ensures that at least 2832 cubic meters per second (100,000 cubic feet per second) flows over the Falls in daylight hours during the tourist season, and half that amount at all other times.

The Falls may be a source of wonder, delight, or even terror. In 1879, Henry Wadsworth Longfellow wrote of Niagara:

I stood within a vision's spell
I saw, I heard. The liquid thunder
Went pouring to its foaming hell
And it fell,
Ever, ever fell
Into the invisible abyss that opened under.

A view of Niagara Falls from the American shore

The brink of the Horseshoe Falls

Niagara Falls is a site of everlasting motion and perpetual change. This grand creation of Nature is always evolving and steadily retreating.

The force of the cascading water continually erodes large sections of rock that fall into the gorge. The top layer of dolomite limestone, directly beneath the rushing water, is a hard surface. But as the tumbling waters cut away the soft shale and sandstone layers below, the limestone layers above collapse.

This erosion moves the face of the Falls gradually upriver. About 12,000 years ago, the Falls was 11 kilometers (7 miles) downstream from its present position. Until the early 1950s, the Falls eroded at a rate of about one meter (3 feet) per year. Since then, water diversion for the power generating stations, and the effect of the International Control Dam that spreads the flow more evenly over the Horseshoe Falls, have combined to slow the rate of erosion considerably. It is now estimated that the brink of the Falls retreats just 36 centimeters (about 1 foot) in ten years.

The Niagara Gorge, extending downstream from the Falls to the foot of the escarpment near the Lewiston-Queenston bridge, traces the path of the receding Falls. The Niagara River is safely navigable for a short distance below the Falls in the Maid of the Mist pool, but as the gorge narrows, the rushing waters seethe and tumble on a tumultuous journey into the Whirlpool. In the ravine below the Whirlpool, the potholes and unusual rock formations are reminders of the Falls' recession.

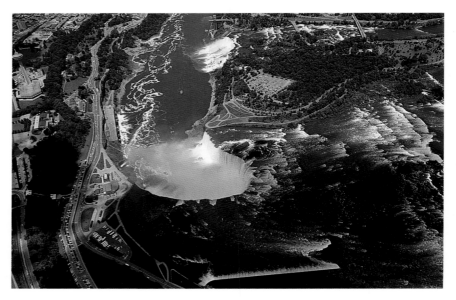

Erosion has moved the Falls 11 kilometers (7 miles) to its present position

Fallen rocks show the forces of erosion at the dewatered American Falls, 1969

The Niagara Gorge was carved by the Falls' recession over many centuries

The brink of the Horseshoe Falls erodes continually, moving it upriver

13

The American Falls

As the Niagara River charges downstream, a cluster of islands separates the flow into separate yet spectacular waterfalls. The American Falls, named for its position on the United States shoreline, extends from Prospect Park on the mainland to Luna Island. A second cascade, the Bridal Veil Falls, makes its narrow course between Luna Island and Goat Island. The Bridal Veil Falls has also been known as the Luna Falls.

The American Falls has a height of 55 meters (180 feet), although the vertical drop is cut in half by the talus slope of fallen rocks at the base. Large rockfalls in 1931 and 1954 dramatically shortened the fall of water. Dewatering the American Falls in 1969 enabled geologists to study the rock formations. It is now believed that the natural flow over the American Falls is not enough to scour away the accumulated fallen rocks at the base. This rock buildup may gradually form a sloping waterfall. It may also stabilize the crest so that the natural recession is virtually halted.

Niagara Falls has inspired writers and artists for centuries. Poet and playwright Oscar Wilde recalled the words of Leonardo da Vinci, who proclaimed that the two most wonderful things in the world are a woman's smile and the motion of mighty waters.

Thomas Jefferson, champion of liberty and third President of the United States, displayed two views of Niagara Falls by John Vanderlyn in the dining room at Monticello. He described the Cascade of Niagara as a landscape "worthy of immortality" and "worth a voyage across the Atlantic."

The brink of the American Falls

Aerial view of the American Falls and narrow Bridal Veil Falls

The Horseshoe Falls

The Horseshoe Falls is the largest waterfall at Niagara, extending from Goat Island to the Canadian shore in the shape of a horseshoe. Ninety percent of the river's volume passes over the Horseshoe Falls, plunging 52 meters (171 feet) into the Maid of the Mist pool below. It is believed that the depth of the riverbed directly beneath the curving crestline is equal to the height of the waterfall itself.

Viewing the Horseshoe Falls in 1842, Charles Dickens wrote, "Niagara was at once stamped upon my heart, an Image of Beauty; to remain there, changeless and indelible, until its pulses cease to beat, forever." His wife's maid was less impressed. She reportedly scoffed, "Nothing but water and too much of that!"

In prose typical of the era, Horatio Parsons' best-selling guidebook of 1836 describes the view of the Falls from the top of Terrapin Tower: "The sublime, arising from obscurity, is here experienced in its greatest force. The eye, unable to discover the bottom of the Falls, or even to penetrate the mist that seems to hang as a veil over the amazing and terrific scene, gives place to the imagination, and the mind is instinctively elevated and filled with majestic dread. Here is 'All that expands the spirit, yet appalls.' "

Table Rock has long been considered an excellent viewing point for visitors to the waterfall. The slight projection that remains today is but a small portion of the remarkably flat ledge of limestone that once extended like a table near the Horseshoe's brink.

Sunrise over the Horseshoe Falls

Terrapin Point at the brink of the Horseshoe Falls

The Horseshoe Falls

Two Nations in Friendship

The border between Canada and the United States is the longest undefended frontier in the world. This boundary line stretches almost five thousand kilometers (more than three thousand miles). A stone erected at Niagara Falls in 1941 describes the remarkable friendship between the two nations as "a lesson in peace to all nations."

The Niagara River became a part of the International Boundary following the American Revolutionary War. Although British and American forces fought bitterly against each other in the War of 1812, the Treaty of Ghent in 1814 left everything as it was before the war, so that captured lands were returned and neither side was victorious. Good statesmanship prevailed and for almost two centuries the two nations have been good neighbors, enjoying peace and cooperation.

Special events occur at the border between Niagara Falls, Ontario, and Niagara Falls, New York. An annual tug of war takes place on the Rainbow Bridge between the police forces of the respective cities. The annual Winter Festival of Lights is a cooperative celebration. And the Thunder over Niagara and Friendship Festival air shows in the sky above the Niagara River are enjoyed on both sides of the border.

On the Whirlpool Rapids Bridge, the site of the first bridge at Niagara, a plaque celebrating one hundred years of service to the people of the United States and Canada describes the four successive bridges on the site as monuments to the friendship existing between these two countries: "They have symbolized to all the world that nations may live at peace with one another."

A New York State Park Police patrol officer on the Niagara Reservation

Royal Canadian Mounted Police, seen at a performance of the Musical Ride in Niagara

Two Nations in Friendship

Four international highway bridges span the border that runs invisibly through the Niagara River. The Rainbow Bridge just north of the Falls was so named because "the rainbow at Niagara Falls denotes peace and happiness and is a symbol of friendship between the two lands whose borders extend along the Niagara River." Local residents make frequent use of the Whirlpool Rapids Bridge, and the Lewiston-Queenston Bridge connects the two historic villages further downstream. The Peace Bridge, linking Buffalo and Fort Erie at the source of the Niagara River, was named in 1929 to commemorate more than one hundred years of peace on the Niagara frontier.

Millions of visitors cross the border at Niagara Falls each year. Customs and Immigration inspectors on the bridges work in cooperation with RCMP marine units and the U.S. Coast Guard, who patrol the International Boundary in the Niagara River.

Before the first bridge appeared in 1848, crossing the Niagara River was a precarious venture, usually involving a long detour. In winter, however, the trip was facilitated by an "ice bridge." Pedestrians made their way over the ice mass spanning the river from shore to shore in the gorge near the base of the Falls. One man's diary in 1835 describes a cross-border trip to buy clover seed. Daily excursions across the ice bridge were very popular until the practice ended in 1912.

As early as 1843, vendors from both countries set up wooden shacks on the ice bridge to sell a variety of souvenirs, refreshments and liquor. It is said that authorities frowned at the ice shanty saloons but were unable to curb their liquor sales. When Canadian police officers appeared, the shacks were shifted easily to the American side, and when American authorities came to inspect, there was a rapid move back to the Canadian side.

The rainbow is a symbol of peace and friendship between Canada and the USA

Until 1912, the ice bridge was a popular route across the border in winter

The Rainbow Bridge spans the Niagara River between the United States and Canada, just north of the Falls

Until the seventeenth century, Niagara was an untamed wilderness inhabited by native Indian tribes. Deep in the interior of a vast continent unexplored by Europeans, the Falls was a familiar site to the Neutral Indians. They grew tobacco, made stone arrowheads, and traded with the neighboring Iroquois and Hurons.

The peaceful Neutrals called the area *Onghiara*. "Thundering waters" is one popular translation for this native word; others believe it means "the great throat," referring to the strait between the vast Great Lakes.

The arrival of Europeans set in motion the gradual destruction of the Indian nations. By the 1600s, explorers and adventurers were swarming out from eastern ports to the south and west, rapidly building trading posts that would later become forts and settlements. The Dutch began trading guns to the Iroquois in exchange for furs and by 1651 the warlike Iroquois had exterminated the Hurons and the Neutrals. In subsequent years, European travellers to Niagara encountered well organized villages of the Iroquois confederacy and began a struggle for domination that lasted more than a century.

No one left a written record of a visit to Niagara Falls until Robert Cavelier, Sieur de la Salle travelled through Niagara in 1678 on his journey to find a water route from Montreal to Mexico. Accompanying La Salle was Father Louis Hennepin, a Recollet priest, who wrote the first eye-witness description of Niagara Falls.

Standing on the "horrible precipice" that is now Queen Victoria Park, Hennepin was awed by the "outrageous noise, more terrible than that of Thunder," of the "vast and prodigious cadence of water" so astonishing "that the Universe does not afford its parallel."

"Father Hennepin at Niagara Falls," a mural by Thomas Hart Benton

Father Hennepin's romantic description of Niagara Falls caused great excitement in Europe when it appeared in his book, *New Discovery,* in 1697. The anonymous engraving that was drawn according to his description became a sensation. Based on Hennepin's exaggerated account, the Falls appear tall and narrow with mountains in the distance. The Bridal Veil Falls are omitted. For the next century and a half, this print inspired artists to draw a variety of views of Niagara Falls, all rendering the scene with similar inaccuracies.

Visitors to Niagara Falls in the eighteenth century likely arrived with false expectations based on Hennepin's description. Hennepin had estimated the height of the waterfall at three times its actual height and some other early visitors judged it to be even higher. "As it is the way of travellers to magnify everything, so has (Hennepin) done with regard to the fall of Niagara," said Peter Kalm in 1750. Scientists like Kalm, a Swedish botanist, soon began making careful measurements of the Falls to correct the errors of the earlier accounts.

When artists began setting up their easels at the Falls, they produced paintings with more accurate proportions. One of the earliest of these artists was Isaac Weld. The Indians in the foreground of his watercolor, *The Falls of Niagara*, are an exotic detail that would have appealed to the public's curiosity about the American wilderness. Europeans were unfamiliar with such wonders as rattlesnakes, eagles, beavers and Indians. Niagara Falls was an imagined site of both beauty and terror.

By the mid-1800s, artistic renderings of the Falls were quite popular. Hippolyte Sebron was one of many famous landscape artists to show the majesty of Niagara Falls to the world.

The first drawing of the Falls, in Hennepin's New Discovery, 1697

"Falls of Niagara," attributed to Isaac Weld, 1796

"Niagara Falls from the Canadian Side," Hippolyte Sebron, ca. 1850

In the 1800s, Niagara Falls was a magnet for artists and popular printmakers. James Cockburn, W. H. Bartlett, W.J. Bennett, August Köllner and John Vanderlyn created the artwork for prints that were made widely available and reasonable enough for the average tourist to afford. Many painters were military topographical artists, trained at Woolwich Academy in England. An officer in each regiment of the British army fulfilled his commission as an artist and left an enduring legacy. A winter scene at the Falls by Sir Richard Levinge depicts one of the full dress parades and mock battles that his regiment regularly enacted for the benefit of Americans watching from across the river.

Perhaps the most famous picture of the mighty cataract, and certainly the most commanding by its sheer scale, is the remarkably realistic *Niagara* by the renowned American landscape artist, Frederic E. Church. When it was first exhibited in New York City in 1857, the public was enthralled. Critics acclaimed it the greatest painting ever made.

Frederic Church had set out to draw the Falls after reading art critic John Ruskin's comment that painting water is "like trying to paint a soul." His work was such a success that even Ruskin declared that the effect of the light on the water was unparalleled, and that he had had to put his hand between the painting and the light from a window to convince himself that the remarkable rainbow was actually painted. Like the Falls itself, the painting is still applauded for its dramatic power and inherent energy.

"The '43rd Light Infantry' as They 'Turn Out' in their Sleighs at the 'Falls of Niagara'," Sir Richard Levinge, 1839

"The Falls of Niagara," James Cockburn, 1833

"Niagara," Frederic E. Church, 1857

Niagara Falls became a favored tourist destination during the 19th century. As it became accessible by the Erie Canal in 1825 and by railway in 1836, its popularity grew. Horatio Parsons proclaimed in *The Book of Niagara Falls* that "the fashionable, the opulent, and the learned congregate here." And the custom of the Niagara honeymoon began to evolve. According to a song that became popular:

Oh, the lovers come a thousand miles,
They leave their home and mother,
Yet when they reach Niagara Falls
They only see each other...

Entrepreneurs made sure the visitors had plenty to do. For a fee, they climbed observation towers such as Street's Pagoda on Cedar Island or the Terrapin Tower on Goat Island. They descended the Biddle Stairs to the base of the American Falls or Thomas Barnett's stairway at Table Rock. A rowboat ferry service operated as early as 1818, crossing the gorge from landings that later became Maid of the Mist docks. A water-powered incline railway ran down the gorge wall to the ferry landing on the American bank by 1845. The Shadow of the Rock dressing room at the foot of the American Falls rented raincoats, and concessions flourished on both banks.

Vacationers in the mid-1800s described a carnival atmosphere at Niagara Falls, with sideshows, dancing monkeys, museums, shops and a barrage of peddlers. Native handicrafts, daguerreotype photos and stereoscopic cards were popular souvenirs. By the 1870s, the "Front," stretching along the Canadian bank from Table Rock to what is now the Oakes Garden Theatre, had become a haven for notorious hucksters and con artists who reportedly swindled and bullied visitors.

The main attraction, however, was the Falls, and visitors enjoyed a view unimpeded by retaining walls, railings, or protective fencing.

A daguerreotype photo concession on Prospect Point, late 1850s

"Table Rock," ca. 1846

*Ferry boats crossing
the Niagara Gorge*

Civil war era visitors to Prospect Point

The incline railway to the ferry landing

An unimpeded view of the Falls, ca. 1860

Goat Island, the famed stretch of land between the American Falls and the Horseshoe Falls, was owned by Peter and Augustus Porter from 1816 to 1885. The Porter brothers were power developers who erected mills on the mainland and on a smaller island, but they had no such plans for Goat Island. Their long tenure on Goat Island likely saved it from development and exploitation. Its unspoiled beauty and grandeur appealed to many an entrepreneur and wealthy visitor, but the Porters would not relinquish their ownership. Even Thomas Jefferson's good friend, the Marquis de Lafayette, is said to have tried to purchase the island as a vacation property. Upon his visit to Goat Island in 1825, he described it as "an aerial garden sustained by clouds and surrounded by thunder."

A toll bridge provided access to Goat Island from the mainland, where Tugby's Bazaar sold curiosities and catered to tourists. Both the toll gate and the popular store were removed when the New York State Reservation was established in 1885. The state government took control of lands bordering the Falls and made Niagara "free to all mankind forever."

In the 1820s the Porters build a wooden walkway from Goat Island to the Terrapin Rocks and extending 3 meters (10 feet) out over the Horseshoe Falls. To further improve the view, they built a stone observation tower in 1833. Shaped like a lighthouse, the Terrapin Tower was a popular point of interest until 1873, when it was declared unsafe and demolished.

In the 1950s, remedial work extended the slowly eroding Terrapin Point with rock fill from the riverbed. A crack in the rock formation at Terrapin Point closed the area to visitors in 1969, however, and it did not reopen to the public until 1983 when the unstable area was blasted away.

The Terrapin Tower and walkway, ca. 1860s

Tugby's Bazaar and the toll gate at the bridge to Goat Island, ca. 1882

"Terrapin Tower – Niagara," Paul Thomas Hanover, 1997

Bridging the Niagara River near the Falls was no simple matter. The great depth of the Niagara River, its furious current and unpredictable ice jams presented formidable obstacles.

A kite flying contest was the ingenious idea of Charles Ellett, an American bridge engineer. When a young boy's kite sailed victoriously across the Niagara Gorge on the second day of the contest, the light rope attached to the kite was used to pull a succession of gradually heavier ropes until a steel cable was finally strung across. Ellett's wooden suspension bridge opened to pedestrian and carriage traffic in the summer of 1848 and became an immediate tourist attraction.

The increasing convergence of railway lines at Niagara Falls necessitated another link across the Niagara River. In 1855, John Roebling spanned the gorge with the world's first suspension bridge to carry railway trains. The double deck bridge was twice the length of any previous railway bridge. Held steady in the heaviest gales by numerous guy wires, the wooden frame structure boasted an upper railway deck and a lower carriage deck of oak and pine planking. In its first year of operation, trains crossed an average of thirty times per day, making it, as one guidebook proclaimed, "the greatest artificial curiosity in America."

A series of bridge improvements and replacements took place as technology inevitably advanced. Eleven bridges were built between 1848 and 1962 at three locations: close to the Falls, near the Whirlpool, and between Lewiston and Queenston. Two bridges were destroyed by the ravages of nature. The Upper Suspension Bridge, built in 1869, succumbed to strong gales twenty years later, and the Honeymoon Bridge of 1889 was toppled by an ice jam in 1938.

A kite flying contest in 1847 to get the first line across for a suspension bridge

Niagara Falls Suspension Bridge, 1848, the first bridge across the Niagara Gorge

John Roebling built the world's first Railway Suspension Bridge at Niagara Falls in 1855

Although steamboats were a boon to early merchants, settlers and visitors to Niagara, and the Erie Canal and Welland Canal provided links around the Falls, railways soon made their mark and became the favored mode of transportation.

By 1837, railways were running daily from Lockport and Buffalo to Niagara Falls, New York. In Canada, the Erie and Ontario horse-drawn railway carried passengers from lakeboats at Queenston landing along the old portage route past the Falls to Chippawa. This route soon extended to Fort Erie and in 1878 became part of the Canada Southern Railway. The stopover at the Falls View Station was its most popular feature.

Roebling's famous Railway Suspension Bridge of 1855 allowed connections between the United States and Canada and railway traffic soared. In the 1850s the Niagara Falls and Ontario Railway ran between Niagara Falls and Lewiston and connected with New York Central trains to Buffalo, New York and Chicago. The Great Western Railway provided service from Niagara Falls to Hamilton and Toronto.

Electric railways were also extremely popular. The Niagara Falls Park and River Railway Company served the west side of the river between the Queenston docks and Chippawa, with stops at Queen Victoria Park. In 1899, a Belt Line was formed, linking the Canadian line with the Great Gorge Route electric railway that ran along the American bank from Lewiston to the Falls.

The ride on the Great Gorge Route was touted as the most spectacular trip of its kind in the world, but was not without mishap. Rock slides occasionally interrupted service until the rubble could be cleared away, and an avalanche of ice tumbled onto one car in 1905, killing the motorman. When heavy rains caused the tracks to sink at one point in 1917, a streetcar toppled over the embankment and into the churning rapids. Fourteen died and many more were injured. Despite this tragedy, the Great Gorge cars continued to operate until 1935, when a huge rock slide buried a long stretch of track.

A Great Gorge Route streetcar in the Niagara Gorge, ca. 1898

Great Gorge Route cars carried 13 million passengers between 1895 and 1935

AMERICAN OLEOGRAPH CO., CHICAGO.

VIEW OF GANADA SOUTHERN TRAIN PASSING NIAGARA FALLS

A stopover at the Falls View Station was a popular feature of railway travel in the late 1800s

The latter years of the 19th century and early years of the 20th century were a time of industrial growth, achievement and unprecedented wealth and prosperity in North America. Vacationers flocked to Niagara Falls from all over the continent and wealthy Europeans often stayed a week or more.

Fashionable hotels and inns sprang up on both banks of the Niagara River to cater to the thousands of sightseers who arrived by automobile, railroad, lake steamers and trolley. The Clifton House, the finest resort on the Canadian riverfront, greeted guests at the site of today's Oakes Garden Theatre. The Cataract House on the American side boasted a huge balcony overlooking the rapids above the American Falls and entertained such notables as Abraham Lincoln, Jenny Lind, Franklin D. Roosevelt and Winston Churchill.

Motor lodges and tourist camps found a growing market in the 1920s and the tourist industry sprawled along the riverbank and into town.

Visitors to Niagara Falls made excursions to a vast array of attractions. One of the earliest was the Burning Spring. An entrepreneur enclosed a natural gas spring in a barrel with a pipe protruding; removing the cork from the pipe and igniting the gas created an aura of great mystery. The Burning Spring was a hit for sixty years until it ran out of gas in 1885. Amid other popular establishments was Thomas Barnett's Niagara Falls Museum. Known for its great collection of natural curiosities and antiquities, the museum opened in 1827 and still exists, despite changes in ownership and moves back and forth across the border.

A tourist camp on Clifton Hill, ca. 1925

Automobiles, a trolley and pedestrians crossing the Honeymoon Bridge, 1918

A stroll on a rocky ledge at the brink of the Horseshoe Falls, with no fencing in sight! Ca. 1884

Royalty, celebrities and heads of state are among the millions of people from all over the world who visit Niagara Falls.

A few months before World War II broke out in Europe, Great Britain's King George VI and Queen Elizabeth enjoyed a six-week tour of Canada. They were greeted by huge crowds at Niagara Falls, Canada, where they dedicated the site of the new Rainbow Bridge. They were not the first British royalty to view the Falls, however, having been preceded by a long line of visitors reaching back as early as 1792, when Prince Edward, the Duke of Kent, toured the area.

World War II brought British Prime Minister Winston Churchill to Canada for a conference in Quebec City with American President Franklin Roosevelt and Russian leader Joseph Stalin. Before returning to England, Churchill and his daughter, Mary, visited the famous Falls.

Shortly following World War II, President Harry Truman made Niagara Falls a stop on his Canadian tour. He concurred with Mayor William Houck of Niagara Falls, Canada, that his visit was a symbol of friendship and peace between two great countries and two great friends. Smiling continually, Truman waved greetings to the enormous crowds he attracted.

The American side of the Falls has had its own share of famous visitors. Several Presidents took in the majestic sight, including Franklin Roosevelt, Jimmy Carter and Gerald Ford. Many years earlier, President Abraham Lincoln made two visits. President McKinley enjoyed a ride on the Great Gorge Route trolley on the morning of the day in 1901 that he was fatally shot in Buffalo, New York. And just weeks before he was elected President, John F. Kennedy made a visit in 1960.

King George VI and Queen Elizabeth view the Falls in 1939

British Prime Minister Winston Churchill at Table Rock, 1943

Presidential candidate John F. Kennedy at Terrapin Point, 1960

President Harry Truman (receiving flowers) and Mayor William Houck, 1947

President McKinley (at center) riding the Great Gorge Route, 1901

A day at Niagara Falls was a great adventure for two young princes of Great Britain and their mother, Princess Diana, in 1991. The highlight of the visit was a ride on the Maid of the Mist. Prince William, 9, and Prince Harry, 7, took turns at the controls in the wheelhouse and blew the horn all the way up the river and back. Their grandparents, Queen Elizabeth II and Prince Philip, visited Niagara Falls forty years earlier during a coast to coast tour of Canada. A crowd estimated at 150,000 greeted the young Princess Elizabeth and Duke of Edinburgh.

Huge crowds also flocked to see the legendary Hollywood film star, Marilyn Monroe, during filming of the movie *Niagara* in 1952. One of the early Technicolor productions for the cinema, *Niagara* showcased the beauty of the Falls, its parklands and attractions. Tourism boomed in the years following the release of the movie, and some say it made Niagara Falls the Honeymoon Capital of the World.

Filming aboard the Maid of the Mist posed a problem that led to an advancement in movie camera technology; the incessant spray of the Falls necessitated development of a protective waterproof casing for the camera. Captain Lawrence McGinn was manager of the Maid of the Mist Steamboat Company at the time. Marilyn Monroe used his office as a dressing room and thrilled employees of the steamboat company by chatting and posing for pictures.

Princess Elizabeth and Prince Philip at Oakes Garden Theatre, 1951

Movie star Marilyn Monroe poses during filming of Niagara, 1952

Princess Diana and sons, Prince Harry, 7, and Prince William, 9, aboard the Maid of the Mist, 1991

Niagara Falls has been an irresistible setting for stunters, and tourists have reveled in such spectacles.

The first of many daredevils was Sam Patch, who came to Niagara in 1829. He built a wooden platform partway down the cliff of Goat Island and announced that he would leap into the seething river below the Falls. Despite heavy rain and poor crowds, Sam Patch jumped from his perch, disappeared for a few moments, and then swam to the rocky shore. Several days later, under better conditions, he repeated the stunt. As he climbed out safely once more, he was heard to say "There's no mistake in Sam Patch." Unfortunately, his next leap, at Genesee Falls, New York, was fatal.

Blondin, a Frenchman who called himself the Prince of Manila, was the first tightrope walker to dazzle crowds at Niagara. He made many trips across the gorge between 1859 and 1861, using a manila rope with guy wires attached to the shore to prevent too much swaying. Blondin crossed first with a balancing pole in his hands, then shackled in chains or blindfolded, and later by bicycle and on stilts. He once lowered a rope to draw up a bottle of champagne from the Maid of the Mist steamboat below, then perched on the rope to take a drink. Later, balancing high above the waters of the gorge, he had a marksman in the boat below him shoot a bullet through the hat he held in his outstretched hand. On another trip, he unwrapped a box camera from his waist and began taking pictures of the astonished crowd that lined the gorge. Blondin's most famous stunt attracted an estimated one hundred thousand spectators as he carried his terrified manager, Harry Colcord, as a rider on his back.

Sam Patch leaps into the Niagara Gorge, 1829 (From a children's book, 1870)

*Blondin on
his tightrope*

Blondin with Harry Colcord on his back, 1860

The Blondin March was composed to honor the daredevil

Daredevils

A procession of tightrope walkers followed Blondin's daring example. William Hunt of Port Hope, Ontario, adopted the stage name Signor Farini and stretched his rope across the gorge in 1860. On one of his daring walks, Farini carried a washing machine halfway across. He lowered a pail to draw water from the river below and began washing ladies handkerchiefs, which he hung out to dry on the uprights and crossbars of his machine.

In 1873 Henry Bellini made a series of dramatic crossings that thrilled spectators. His performances encouraged Stephen Peer to make an impromptu display on Bellini's rope. In a later venture out onto a steel cable at night, Stephen Peer fell to his death.

The first woman to cross the Niagara Gorge on a tightrope was Maria Spelterina. The Italian signorina made a spectacular walk in 1876 with peach baskets strapped to her feet. She crossed once blindfolded, once with her wrists and ankles manacled, and once with her head inside a paper bag.

Despite an attempt by Queen Victoria Park Commissioners to prohibit rope walkers from anchoring their ropes and wires to the gorge wall, the stunts continued. Samuel Dixon crossed over the most turbulent part of the Whirlpool Rapids in 1891. When he reached the American side, his friends hid his balancing pole in the woods and his distraught wife begged him not to make the return trip. But the show went on. Dixon made several crossings, once laying at full length on the wire and once walking with his legs in a hoop.

Clifford Calverley pushed a wheelbarrow across his steel cable in 1892 and set a speed record a year later by crossing the gorge in just 2 minutes and thirty-five seconds. Three years later, 21 year-old James Hardy became the youngest person to make a crossing. He was also the last person to do so for many years, and the great era of the tightrope walkers at Niagara drew to a close.

Farini and his washing machine, 1860

Bellini crossing the gorge, 1873

Bellini on his cable, 1873

Samuel Dixon with his legs in a hoop, 1891

Maria Spelterina with peach baskets on her feet, 1876

Clifford Calverley and his wheelbarrow, 1892

As tightrope walkers performed stunts high above the Niagara River, other daredevils challenged the raging waters below.

The first was Captain Matthew Webb in 1883, a swimmer of worldwide renown and conqueror of the English Channel. Determined to swim through the Whirlpool Rapids to Lewiston, Webb dove into the Niagara River near the Maid of the Mist landing, wearing only silk swimming trunks. He swam into the savage current, then vanished and reappeared several times. Webb raised his head at the mouth of the Whirlpool, but then, tragically, he was pulled into the vortex. His body was not found for four days.

A *Saturday Review* editorial following Webb's death observed "Nothing was to be gained by success – if success had been possible – beyond a temporary notoriety and the applause of a mob." Yet other daredevils seemed encouraged, not discouraged, by Webb's failure. William Kendall, a Boston policeman, attempted the same feat in 1886, but wore a life preserver. He negotiated the Whirlpool Rapids successfully.

Also drawn to the turbulent waters of the gorge, Carlisle Graham crawled into a wooden barrel in 1886 and successfully shot the rapids from Niagara Falls to Lewiston, New York. Despite extreme dizziness from the continual spinning and tossing of the barrel, Graham repeated the trip a few weeks later with his head protruding from the top of the barrel. This stunt permanently affected his hearing.

Martha Wagenfuhrer borrowed Graham's barrel for a turbulent ride in 1901. Caught in the Whirlpool, she rolled and circled for an hour before being rescued. The next day, Maude Willard used the same barrel to ride the rapids. Spinning out of reach of rescuers for many hours in the Whirlpool, she suffocated; her pet dog cut off her air supply by pressing its nose into the only air hole. The dog survived. Willard's tragic ride ended the antics in the gorge rapids for many years to come.

Carlisle Graham conquered the Whirlpool Rapids in a barrel, 1886

Martha Wagenfuhrer rode the rapids in Graham's barrel, 1901

Matthew Webb attempted to swim through the Whirlpool Rapids, 1883

William Kendall's life preserver aided his successful swim, 1886

Riding over the Horseshoe Falls in a barrel became an overnight sensation when Annie Taylor had a notion to do just that in 1901. The sixty-three-year-old school teacher from Bay City, Michigan, was an unlikely adventurer. She could not swim and she had never been an athlete or a professional performer.

An inventive woman, Annie Taylor fitted a wooden barrel with cushions, an air pump and a leather harness to hold her in place. A blacksmith's anvil in the bottom provided ballast to keep the cask floating upright. Two men towed her out into the upper river and then cut her loose from their boat. They chose a spot in the upper rapids where the current seemed to aim directly at the middle of the Horseshoe, hoping to avoid the giant boulders at either side of the base of the Falls.

To the astonishment of thousands of breathless onlookers, the barrel dove over the brink and out of sight, then bobbed up and drifted toward the Canadian side of the gorge. Frantic rescuers pried the lid open; a waving hand emerged. The brave woman survived the plunge.

Dubbing herself the "Queen of the Mist," Annie Taylor anticipated great fame and fortune. Although she gained prominence as the first barrel rider to go over the Falls, she never achieved financial rewards and she died penniless.

"I would caution anyone against attempting the feat," said Annie. "I will never go over the Falls again. I would sooner walk up to the mouth of a cannon knowing it was going to blow me to pieces than make another trip over the Falls."

Annie Taylor, the first person to go over the Horseshoe Falls in a barrel

Annie Taylor looks out from her barrel as rivermen prepare to tow her into the upper rapids and cut her loose, 1901

Daredevils

Annie Taylor's daring feat attracted others who gambled with death by plunging over the Horseshoe Falls. Bobby Leach, a British saloonkeeper, made the trip in 1911 in a steel barrel. Bruised and injured, but more resilient than the dents in his barrel, he spent twenty-three weeks recuperating in hospital.

Also successful was Jean Lussier in 1928. With common sense and ingenuity, he designed a rubber ball made of 32 inner tubes with a steel frame. Lussier emerged smiling and without a scratch after his ball bobbed about in the rapids and then skipped out over the brink.

William Fitzgerald, a research scientist from New York City, designed a ball similar to Lussier's for a plunge over the Falls. Adopting the alias of Nathan Boya, he emerged triumphantly after his unannounced plunge in 1961. When Niagara Parks Police reached his ball-shaped vehicle in the pool below the Falls, he was struggling to close the hatch which had sprung open. He did not realize that he had already made the gigantic plunge.

Charles Stephens and George Stathakis were less fortunate in their attempts to challenge the Falls. Despite warnings from Bobby Leach and a local riverman, Stephens strapped an anvil to his feet inside his crude barrel and was killed when he struck the pool at the base of the Falls in 1920. Ten years later, Stathakis lost his life by suffocation when his heavy oak barrel was caught behind the Falls for fourteen hours.

Bobby Leach challenged the Horseshoe Falls in this steel barrel, 1911

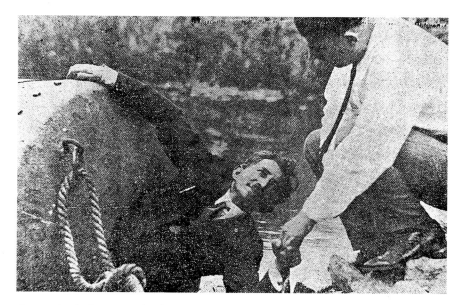

George Stathakis enters his barrel for its ill-fated ride, 1930

Triumphant Jean Lussier in his hometown of Niagara Falls, NY, 1928

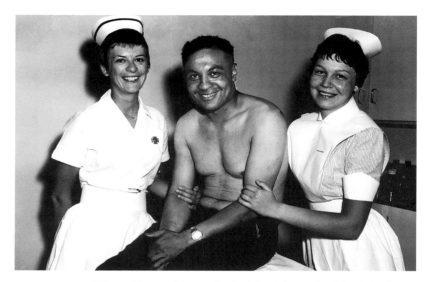

William Fitzgerald was checked for injury after his 1961 plunge

Niagara rivermen recover Fitzgerald's ball, 1961

The saga of the William "Red" Hill family of Niagara Falls, Canada, is filled with as much heroism, daring, mishap and tragedy as the history of the river itself. The exploits of Red Hill and his sons are as legendary as their love of the treacherous and turbulent Niagara River.

Red Hill was a knowledgeable and sensible riverman. From the age of 13, when he helped free Annie Taylor from her barrel in 1901, Red Hill was a keen participant in the life of the river. In 1918, Red scurried along a rope to rescue two men marooned on a scow in the upper rapids. Over the years, he saved 28 people from the Niagara River, pulled out 177 bodies, and lost no opportunity to save stranded swans, geese, ducks and deer. Three times he rode through the Whirlpool Rapids in a barrel. On his third trip, his oldest son, Red Hill Junior, swam out with a rope to save him from the leaking cask that was caught spinning in the Whirlpool.

Sons Red Junior, Major, Corky and Wes continued their father's lifesaving efforts, helping to rescue stranded people and boats and recovering hundreds of bodies from the gorge. Although Red Senior had been convinced that a plunge over the Falls was insanity, his sons Major and Red Junior had ideas of their own. In 1948 Major shot the lower rapids in a barrel, and two years later became the first Hill to attempt to go over the Falls. Major's barrel caught in the rocks of the upper rapids, however, aborting the trip.

In 1951, Red Junior planned to conquer the Horseshoe Falls in a loosely tied row of truck inner tubes, which he called "The Thing." Family friend, Pat Simon, cautioned that it was unsafe and there was no possible way to survive the trip, but to no avail. Red Junior lost his life when the contraption broke into pieces during the plunge. As riverman Ken Sloggett remarked, "he underestimated the power of the Falls."

Red Hill in the doorway of his shop on Bridge Street, ca. 1940

Red Hill rode the Whirlpool Rapids in Stathakis' barrel, 1930

Major Hill shot the Whirlpool Rapids in a steel barrel, 1948

Red Hill Junior in "The Thing," 1951

Red Hill Junior's trip over the Falls ended in tragedy

Daredevils

Despite laws forbidding acts of stunting in the Niagara River, several modern day daredevils have defied the power of Niagara's torrent and taken a ride over the Horseshoe Falls. In 1984, Karel Soucek was the first Canadian to do so, followed a year later by 22-year old Steven Trotter, who was the youngest. David Munday made his first trip in 1985 and another in 1993. Following the 1989 example of Peter DeBernardi and Geoffrey Petkovich, who were the first pair to ride in the same barrel, Steven Trotter made the plunge again in 1995 with a friend, Lori Martin.

The barrels used in the 1980s and 1990s showed great improvement over Annie Taylor's crude wine cask of 1901. Constructed of steel or plastic, most had foam insulation or similar padding. Some contained oxygen tanks and radio equipment to communicate with friends on shore. Cautiously avoiding detection by Niagara Parks Police, these daredevils transported their concealed barrels to a spot above the Horseshoe Falls and made a swift launch into the rapids. Their stunts could not be advertised because of their illegality, so unsuspecting sightseers caught an exclusive glimpse of their daring acts. In one case, tourists helped launch a barrel over the railing when the truck conveying it proved to be lower than the fence.

All of these stunters survived the plunge. Emerging from their barrels with only minor scrapes and bruises, all were required to pay fines for illegal stunting, and Steven Trotter spent two weeks in jail. Trotter remarked that the plunge was like dropping in an elevator without a cable, and Lori Martin commented that riding in the barrel felt like being inside a clothes dryer.

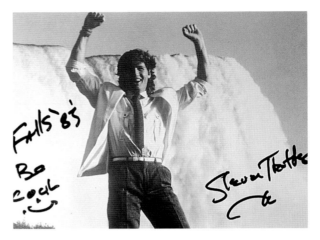

Triumphant Steven Trotter in 1985

Karel Soucek's steel barrel, 1984

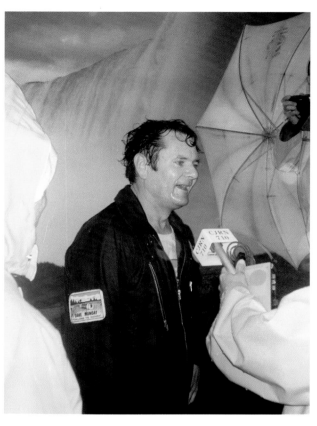

David Munday after his first plunge, 1985

DeBernardi and Petkovich's barrel at the brink, 1989

The erosion of the Niagara Gorge walls is a natural and ongoing process. Over many thousands of years, erosion has moved the crest of the Falls upriver to its present location, creating the spectacular, steep walled gorge of the lower Niagara River. Inescapably, this erosion has been responsible for dramatic changes and tragedy.

Long considered the best vantage point for visitors to the Falls, Table Rock was once a remarkably large and flat limestone ledge that jutted out like a table at the brink of the Horseshoe Falls. Pieces of the rock began falling in 1818. In 1850, a cab driver had just unhitched his horses for their noon-day feeding when a resounding crack spelled disaster. The carriage and the great projecting rock tumbled into the gorge as the driver scrambled to safety. The remnants of Table Rock were blasted away in 1935 to ensure the safety of visitors.

Prospect Point, a popular viewing station on the American side of the gorge, met a similar fate. In July 1954, park officials noticed a crack in the pavement indicating an inevitable rockfall. Within hours, more than 185,000 tons of rock dropped into the gorge. Ten days later, crews used a power shovel to loosen a 2700-ton mass that failed to fall earlier.

The Schoellkopf Station, a multimillion dollar hydro-electric power plant of the Niagara Mohawk Power Corporation built in 1923, was located at the base of the gorge in Niagara Falls, New York. On June 7, 1956, workers saw water trickling into the powerhouse through newly formed cracks. They sandbagged leaks and propped a door open as a precaution, but destruction was imminent. When the walls began cracking, forty workers raced for the door; all escaped but one. In a fifteen minute period, three separate rock slides dropped about 120,000 tons of rock onto the powerhouse, completely destroying two sections of the plant, and burning out the generators in the oldest section, which remained intact.

Rockfall at Prospect Point, 1954

A blasting crew works to clean up the Prospect Point rockfall

The Fall of Table Rock, 1850

A rock slide collapsed the Schoellkopf Station, 1956

Water destined for the turbines poured through the plant for several days

When the winter sun glistens off the ice mounds in the gorge below the Falls, and ice crystals turn railings and trees into a magical wonderland, it is hard to imagine the awesome destructive power of that ice and the tragedy it has wrought.

The unyielding force of ice brought down the famous Honeymoon Bridge on January 27, 1938. Also known as the Upper Steel Arch Bridge and the Falls View Bridge, it spanned the river near the site of the present Rainbow Bridge. Tremendous quantities of ice that floated into the Niagara River from Lake Erie had piled high about the bridge abutments. When the girders bent and the rivets were heard to snap, traffic was banned. Within hours, the bridge crumbled and fell. The twisted frame rested on the ice for weeks before the ice pack released part of it to the riverbed below and carried the rest of the structure downstream.

Years earlier, the ice bridge in the gorge suddenly broke away with tragic consequences. February 4, 1912 was a clear and cold day, and as had been the custom for more than seventy-five years, people ventured out onto the huge jam of ice in front of the Falls to enjoy the thrills of winter, visit the ice shacks or cross the border on well worn paths. Without warning, the ice began to move. Terrified people scrambled to the shore.

Four people were caught on moving ice floes. River-man Red Hill pulled Ignatius Roth to safety, but Roth's friend, Burrell Hecock, had turned back to help Mr. and Mrs. Eldridge Stanton. The trio became separated from shore and drifted downriver. Quick thinking men lowered ropes from the bridges. Hecock grasped one but lost it, and Stanton's frantic attempts to secure a rope were in vain. The ice broke up as it carried them into the seething rapids and all three drowned. This tragedy ended all activity on the ice bridge. Officials enforced a permanent ban on walking upon the lower gorge ice.

An ice jam collapsed the Honeymoon Bridge, January 27, 1938

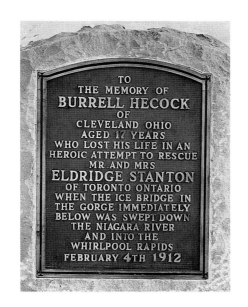

Burrell Hecock memorial plaque

Burrell Hecock on an ice floe, drifting helplessly to his death, 1912

The ice bridge on February 4, 1912, just hours before it broke apart

There can be no waters more treacherous for navigation than the upper rapids and Whirlpool Gorge of the Niagara River. Many vessels have succumbed to the mighty turbulence, others have given their occupants the ride of their lives.

In 1861, Captain Joel Robinson and two crew members undertook the seemingly impossible task of delivering the second Maid of the Mist steamboat through the perilous lower Niagara River to Lake Ontario, after it had been sold at auction. Spectators jammed the suspension bridge and shore. The boat shot into the rapids with such force that the men were unable to hold onto the wheel and the smokestack was torn off. Robinson seized the helm in the Whirlpool and managed to avoid its vortex, sending the boat at tremendous speed towards Queenston, where it arrived safely.

In the upper river, a steel scow broke loose from its tug in 1918 and was heading straight towards the Falls. The two men on board seemed doomed in the relentless current, but their efforts to open the bottom dumping door succeeded in grounding the scow on a rocky ledge. The men spent a harrowing 29 hours on board. The U.S. Coast Guard used a cannon to shoot out a rescue line. Riverman Red Hill moved hand over hand along the line to help bring the men to safety. The scow remains marooned to this day.

The American steamer Caroline also met its fate in the upper rapids. It was used to ferry men and supplies to William Lyon Mackenzie, a leader of the reform movement in Upper Canada. In 1837 he had established headquarters on Navy Island in the Niagara River, a short distance above the Falls, seeking arms, ammunition and volunteers to aid his struggle against British tyranny. The Canadian militia retaliated by ejecting the crew from the Caroline, cutting the ship loose and setting it on fire. Mackenzie and his patriots quickly withdrew.

Captain Robinson navigated the Maid of the Mist through the Whirlpool, 1861

A steel scow, stranded in the upper rapids since 1918

"The Caroline Steam Boat Precipitated over the Falls of Niagara," engraving, ca. 1838

Boy's Nightmare Plunge screamed the headlines. Some called it luck, some called it fate, and some called it a miracle. On July 9, 1960, seven-year-old Roger Woodward survived a trip through the upper rapids and over the Horseshoe Falls, wearing only his swimming suit and a life jacket.

Jim Honeycutt, a family friend, took Roger and his 17-year-old sister, Deanne Woodward, for a boat ride in the upper Niagara River. They passed the International Control Dam and were approaching Goat Island when the outboard motor failed. Waves capsized the boat and the three terrified occupants were thrown into the raging rapids.

Deanne recalls tossing about in the churning and frothing waters, often submerged to depths so deep that it was pitch black. She kept her eyes open and held her breath each time she was hurtled beneath the surface. Two sightseers on Terrapin Point were able to pull Deanne to safety, but none of the horrified onlookers could reach the others. Honeycutt tragically disappeared and his body was found four days later, but Roger Woodward survived.

Clad in his protective life vest, Roger bounced through the rapids and catapulted out over the Horseshoe Falls. He dropped into the swirling maelstrom below and bobbed up to the surface like a cork. His bright orange jacket attracted the attention of the crew on the Maid of the Mist. With the turbulence and current pulling the boy away, it was a few terrifying minutes before the vessel was close enough to rescue him. Passengers watched helplessly as the first two attempts to throw out a life ring fell short of their target. The third throw was successful and the boy was pulled to safety. It was the first time that the life rings on board had been used in more than 100 years of operation. Roger Woodward miraculously survived his nightmarish plunge over the Horseshoe Falls with only a few bruises and scratches.

Roger Woodward awaits rescue at the base of the Horseshoe Falls

Roger Woodward clings to a life ring thrown from the Maid of the Mist

Winter at the Falls

Winter is a time of spectacular beauty and enchantment at Niagara Falls. Snow and freezing rain combine with the mist that rises from the mighty cataracts to create dramatic scenery by the Falls. Huge glittering icicles hang from projecting rocks. Tree branches extend dazzling crystalline fingers. Frozen spray covers railings and lamp posts, creating the aura of a magic land. Ice mountains that form at the base of the Falls give the winter scene a lunar quality.

The naturally forming mass of ice in the pool and the gorge below the Falls is known as the ice bridge. This solid span has considerable strength and great depth. It usually begins to form in January each year and may last two to three months, depending on the severity of the winter. As the ice cover on Lake Erie breaks up, blocks of ice float down the Niagara River and over the Falls to be consolidated into the ice mass. Some winters the ice bridge is flat with few irregularities in its surface, while in other years it is jagged with high ridges and deep crevasses.

A visit to the Falls in the winter of 1854 made such an impression on Bayard Taylor that he described the sight as "a landscape of sparkling silver...infinitely more brilliant than in summer....With each succeeding visit, Niagara has grown in height, in power, in majesty, in solemnity; but (in winter) I have seen its climax of beauty."

Above the Horseshoe Falls

The ice bridge in the Maid of the Mist pool

The Horseshoe Falls

The American Falls and Prospect Park

The ice bridge in the Niagara Gorge

Enjoying a day on the ice bridge was once an eagerly anticipated winter activity. The unique winter scenery at the Falls created a playground that was much enjoyed by tourists and residents of the area. Sledding, climbing or skating on the ice mountains at the base of the Falls was exhilarating exercise. A Salvation Army band performed Sunday services on the ice below Prospect Point. Enterprising shopkeepers dragged wooden shanties out onto the ice. Their string of shacks followed a path from shore to shore between the ferry landings, circling around crevasses and ice mounds. Visitors to the shanties bought tintype photographs, souvenirs, and refreshments. Some of the more popular shanties were saloons selling hard liquor.

So popular was the pastime of walking on the ice bridge that streetcar lines and railroad companies offered special excursion trains to bring tourists from out of town. A newspaper account in 1888 estimated the crowd one Sunday at 20,000 people. The widespread fascination with this novelty ended in 1912 when the ice bridge suddenly broke up, sweeping three tourists to their death.

During particularly harsh winters, the frozen river has reduced the American Falls to a mere trickle. Brave sightseers have been known to venture out onto the ice at the brink. In an unusual occurrence in 1948, a giant ice jam in the upper Niagara River essentially stopped any flow over the Horseshoe Falls for more than 24 hours.

The incline railway and chalet below Prospect Point, ca. 1890s

Shanties on the ice bridge, ca. 1900

A great mound of ice buried Prospect Point, 1904

"Coasting below the American Falls," 1880

Walking the ice mounds below the frozen American Falls, ca. 1896

Winter at the Falls

In the late 1800s and early 1900s, Niagara Falls was the scene of spectacular winter activities. Descending a stairway or the water-powered incline railway from Prospect Point to the base of the gorge, sightseers explored the magical winter transformation at the Cave of the Winds. They marveled at the crystalline ice mounds and giant icicles, posing for some unique photographs. At that time, an opening led to a natural cavern behind the Bridal Veil Falls. This cave collapsed in 1920, preventing further access to the vantage point depicted in early prints.

Those who ventured away from the shoreline onto the slippery ice formation at the foot of the American Falls found the footing could be precarious. Skating was quite popular and at one point, a notice advised: "No one allowed thereon unless equipped with ice skates or ice creepers."

In the winter of 1899, an Ice Palace was erected in the New York State Reservation at the corner of River Way and Niagara Street. Its thick walls were constructed entirely of crystal ice; it was illuminated by electricity generated from the power of the Falls.

Skating on the ice bridge, ca. 1904

The Ice Palace at Niagara Falls, New York, January 1899

Behind the Bridal Veil Falls, ca. 1896

At the Cave of the Winds in winter, 1896

Niagara Folklore

Few legends are as colorful or as pervasive as that of Lelawala, the Maid of the Mist.

For the native inhabitants, the Falls was a sacred place and the home of Hinu, the Thunder God, who lived in a cave behind the Falls. It is said that the beautiful maiden, Lelawala, paddled over the Falls in a canoe brimming with flowers and ripe fruit. Her distraught father, Chief Eagle Eye, climbed into his canoe and followed her. Lelawala disappeared into the foam and mists of the cataract, but in her descent she was caught in the arms of the Thunder God. She became suspended forever between life and death and remains there still, the Maid of the Mist.

Various versions of the story abound. Some say she was escaping an unhappy betrothal. Others say she was part of an annual spring ritual, sacrificed to the native god to spare her fellow tribesmen from catastrophe. In yet another story, the god Hinu, who rescued Lelawala, taught her about a great snake responsible for bringing illness and death to her village, and then killed the enormous serpent, which wedged itself in the rocks of the Niagara River and gave the Horseshoe Falls its shape.

None of the tales of Lelawala are mentioned in any of the carefully kept records of the Jesuit missionaries who mingled with the native inhabitants of Niagara. The story may be the creative fabrication of tourist guides in the early 1800s. The Maid of the Mist legend has persisted, however, for more than 150 years and it is likely to remain a popular part of the folklore of Niagara Falls.

For those who look closely, the face of the Thunder God, Hinu, appears in the Falls

"The Redman's Fact: The Maiden Sacrifice," ca. 1891

"The White Man's Fancy: The Maid of the Mist," ca. 1891

Niagara Folklore

The legendary Hermit of Niagara was an astonishing spectacle for viewers of the Falls in the early nineteenth century. Living alone in a log cabin on Goat Island, the Hermit took daily walks back and forth on a piece of timber that was lodged in the end of the Terrapin walkway and projected out over the Horseshoe Falls. Observers reported that he danced and pirouetted and would sometimes hang carelessly from the timber, suspended by his hands or legs. In his bare feet and dark gown, with long hair flying in the wind, he was a great curiosity.

Niagara residents and tourists were fascinated with the mysterious figure. Visitors to his cabin found him painting, writing poetry or playing one of his musical instruments. It is said that he bathed in the upper rapids and swam about at the base of the Falls, but the brink of the cataract at Terrapin Point was his favorite haunt. The Hermit was seen almost daily for two years until he drowned in 1831; his body was recovered in the Whirlpool. It later became known that the Hermit's name was Francis Abbott and that he was the son of a well-to-do family in Plymouth, England.

The name of Goat Island is also the subject of local folklore. John Stedman, a British contractor for the portage on the east bank of the river, moved a number of animals onto the island in 1770 to protect them from wolves and bears on the mainland. It is said that only a solitary male goat survived the harsh winter. Stedman's associates promptly dubbed the place Goat Island. Even though a map accompanying the Treaty of Ghent showed it as Iris Island in 1814, the popular local name persisted, and it is still known as Goat Island.

"The Hermit of Niagara." An original watercolor by Laurel Campbell, 1997

"American Fall from Goat Island," W. J. Bennett, ca. 1830

More than two centuries ago, settlers built sawmills and grist mills along the upper Niagara River, turning their paddle wheels with the rushing water from the river. By 1875, industrial pioneers were building water powered factories along the high bank of the Niagara Gorge. Water diverted from the upper Niagara River ran through an open canal to turn the waterwheels that powered the machinery. The water then spilled over the face of the cliff into the lower Niagara River.

A new era dawned, however, when the discoveries of Nikola Tesla, scientist and inventor, were applied for the first time in the construction of electrical power generating plants at Niagara Falls. Jacob Schoellkopf built the first electric generating unit on the American side of the river in 1881. It supplied electricity for a paper company, some small factories, and street lighting in Niagara Falls, New York. In Canada, a small plant just above the Horseshoe Falls began generating electricity in 1893 to power an electric railway between the villages of Queenston and Chippawa. And by 1895, the first large-scale hydroelectric plant in the world, the Edward Dean Adams Station, began operating in the gorge at Niagara Falls, New York.

All over the world, people hailed the power plants at Niagara Falls as a wonderful demonstration of human mastery over the forces of nature. H. G. Wells was so impressed with the dynamos and galleries of the Niagara Falls Power Company in 1906 that he pronounced them profoundly more beautiful than the Cave of the Winds. He declared that power development at Niagara Falls was his "ultimate image of the technological sublime."

In the twentieth century, Niagara's cheap and convenient source of electrical power made it a prime location for power generation. The Niagara River is today one of the world's greatest sources of hydroelectric power. Massive power plants on both sides of the river transform the energy of the rushing water into electricity.

Water powered factories lined the American bank of the gorge in the late 1800s

A statue on Goat Island honors Nikola Tesla, inventor of modern electrical energy

"Six Million Wild Horses" celebrates man's achievement in harnessing the energy of Niagara Falls to create electrical power. Electricity was first measured in horsepower.

Power plants sprang up along the Niagara River as North Americans entered the twentieth century. A group of American capitalists formed the Canadian Niagara Power Company and built a powerhouse in 1905 on the Canadian mainland behind Cedar Island. It was built for the transmission and sale of electrical power outside of Niagara Falls, Ontario. The plant was named the William Birch Rankine Generating Station in honor of the American lawyer whose interest in power development led to the construction of this powerhouse as well as two across the border.

Operated by the Canadian Niagara Power Company, the Rankine Generating Station is the only hydroelectric plant near the Falls that is privately owned. It remained under American ownership for almost a century. In 1996, however, a Canadian company, Fortis, became an equal partner with the previous owner, Niagara Mohawk Power Corporation.

The Rankine powerhouse has a generating capacity of 74,600 kilowatts. The forebay of the plant is the portion of the river channel that circles around Cedar Island. Its tailrace water flows through a tunnel into the lower Niagara River just below the Horseshoe Falls.

Nearby, the magnificent Italian Renaissance style building that flanks the rapids just above the Falls was also a powerhouse. Built by the Electrical Development Company of Ontario, the fine building of Indiana limestone was commonly called the Toronto Power Station. It stands on an area of reclaimed riverbed. The site was once an area of very turbulent rapids known as the Tempest and the Whitehorse Rapids.

The Toronto Power Station produced 25-cycle electricity. First delivering power in 1906 but not completed until 1913, it had an installed capacity of 102,500 kilowatts. The station closed in 1974.

Penstock (Rankine)

Generators (Rankine)

Rankine Generating Station has operated since 1905

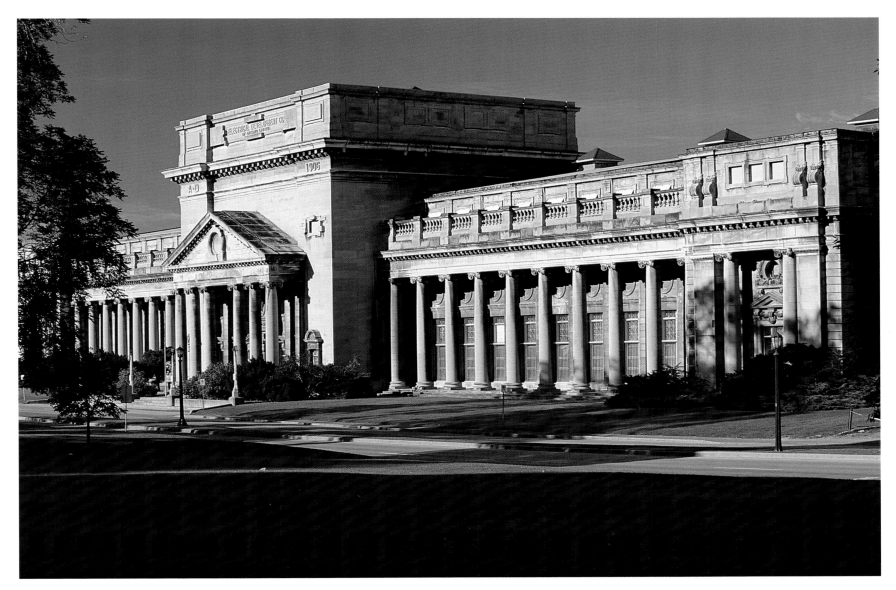

The Toronto Power Station operated from 1906 until it closed in 1974

The Ontario Power Generating Station has been operating since 1905 at the base of the Niagara Gorge near the Horseshoe Falls. Built with the aid of American financing, it was purchased in 1917 by the Hydro-Electric Power Commission which later became known as Ontario Hydro. It was the first power station owned by the public utility in Ontario. With nine units in service today, its generating capacity is 74,000 kilowatts.

Water gathered in the Niagara River above Dufferin Islands passes through a screen house and gate house. Logs and ice are kept from entering the forebay, and shut-off gates regulate the volume of water that passes from the forebay. Three large tunnels carry water beneath Queen Victoria Park to penstocks leading to the powerhouse below the Falls.

An international agreement controls the flow of water to the generating station. The International Control Dam extends out into the Niagara River from the Canadian shore just above the Falls. Its 18 gates open and close to regulate the flow of water or ice that goes over the Falls and to generating stations.

Niagara's notorious ice jams inflicted damage on the Ontario Power Generating Station in 1909 and again in 1938. The powerhouse filled with ice. To avoid potentially destructive ice buildup, Canadian and American power utilities send out icebreakers that work together on the upper Niagara River during the winter months.

An inspection party inside a concrete water diversion tunnel, July 1910

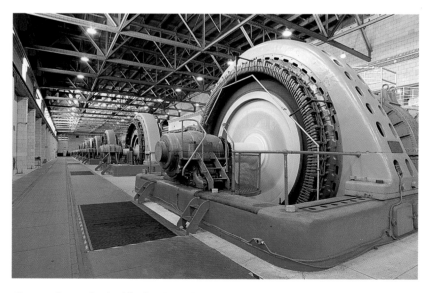

Generating units inside the Ontario Power Generating Station

The Ontario Power Generating Station at the base of the gorge below Queen Victoria Park

The growing demand for electricity in the early twentieth century spurred the construction of a large-scale hydroelectric generating plant on the Canadian side of the Niagara River near Queenston. An open canal was constructed to divert water from Chippawa, above the Horseshoe Falls, through the City of Niagara Falls to the plant's forebay, a basin on the escarpment above the Niagara River. Sir Adam Beck 1 Generating Station began operating in 1922. With ten generating units and a capacity of 470,000 kilowatts, it was for many years the largest hydroelectric plant in the world.

Increased electricity production during World War II proved that more water flow could be diverted for power generation purposes without disturbing the scenic beauty of the Falls. As a result, Ontario Hydro began construction on a new generating station adjacent to Sir Adam Beck 1. Twin parallel tunnels were built directly beneath the city to carry water from Chippawa to the forebay. Completed in 1958, Sir Adam Beck 2 Generating Station has 16 generating units and an installed capacity of 1,290,000 kilowatts.

A pumping generating station contributes an additional 120,000 kilowatts of generating capacity. The station's six pumps draw water from the power canal for storage in a reservoir during periods of low demand, but reverse the flow to generate electricity when demand peaks. The station was the first of its kind when it opened in 1958.

To accommodate ever increasing demand, studies have been completed for a third generating station with a 700,000 kilowatt capacity. Twin tunnels constructed beneath the existing tunnels would divert water to a new station located underground between the first plant and the Lewiston-Queenston Bridge.

Generating units inside Sir Adam Beck 2 Generating Station

Sir Adam Beck 2 Generating Station is Ontario's largest hydroelectric station

The Sir Adam Beck power stations flank the Niagara River below the Pumping Generating Station and its reservoir

New York State's largest producer of electricity is the Niagara Power Project on the lower Niagara River. Operated by the New York Power Authority, the main generating facility and a pump-generating plant have a generating capacity of more than 2.4 million kilowatts of electricity. When the project began producing electricity in 1961, it was the largest hydropower facility in the western world.

The Robert Moses Niagara Power Plant is the Project's main generating facility. It was constructed under the leadership of New York's "Master Builder" and named in his honor. Water intakes in the upper Niagara River draw water into twin concrete conduits that run beneath the City of Niagara Falls to the forebay in Lewiston. Steel penstocks encased in a massive slope of reinforced concrete carry the rushing water to 13 turbine-generators in the main power plant at the base of the gorge. A refurbishment program is underway at the Robert Moses Niagara Power Plant to improve the efficiency of the 13 generating units and increase peak power production.

On the height of land above the main plant, the Lewiston Pump-Generating Plant draws water from the east end of the project's forebay into a 1900-acre reservoir during periods of low electricity demand. In peak hours, the twelve pumping units are reversed to operate as turbine generators producing up to 300,000 kilowatts of electricity.

The Robert Moses Niagara Power Plant on the lower Niagara River

Installation work on a new turbine

A generator undergoing modifications

Centering a stator during upgrade

The New York Power Authority's Niagara Power Project

An organized public campaign arose on both sides of the border in the late 1800s seeking government action to preserve the beauty of the Falls area. Although no North American government had ever appropriated privately owned land to make it available for public use, landscape architect Frederick Olmstead and artist Frederic Church spearheaded a movement known as "Free Niagara" to prevent industrialization and commercialization of the premier natural landscape of the Falls. As a result, a state reservation was established in 1885 in Niagara Falls, New York, and the work began of tearing down signs, fences, towers and buildings that lined the riverbank. In the same year, spurred on by the urging of Lord Dufferin, Canada's first Governor-General, the government of Ontario enacted legislation to create its first provincial parkland at Niagara Falls. Private property was expropriated along the notorious "Front" and three years later the restored area opened to the public, named Queen Victoria Park in honor of the reigning British monarch.

On the American shore, eleven islands and Prospect Park on the mainland make up the Niagara Reservation, the oldest state park in the United States. On the opposite bank lies Queen Victoria Park, with its velvety green gardens, colorful flowers and trees continually refreshed by the spray from the Falls.

The management of the public lands adjacent to the Falls is a continual balancing act between the interests of preservationists and commercial developers. Naturalists suffered a tremendous setback with the construction of the four-lane Robert Moses Parkway through Niagara Reservation lands on the east side of the lower gorge in the 1960s. In Ontario, the Niagara Parks Commission manages more than 1512 hectares (3735 acres) by the Falls and along the Niagara River corridor from Lake Erie to Lake Ontario, actively working to preserve and enhance the natural beauty of the Falls area for the enjoyment of visitors.

The Niagara Reservation is the oldest state park in the United States

The lush gardens of Queen Victoria Park are an ideal vantage point for viewing the Falls

The Falls area is renowned for its magnificent gardens and floral displays.

The Floral Clock, just north of the Adam Beck power plant, is an intriguing arrangement of 24,000 plants forming an immense timepiece. Westminster chimes intone the quarters and strike the hour. Each spring planting is a new and innovative design for the face of the Floral Clock.

The Oakes Garden Theatre at the north end of Queen Victoria Park was created by the Niagara Parks Commission on land donated by Sir Harry Oakes. It is a unique formal garden with a curved pergola, open pavilions, sloping terraces and a rock garden. The world famous Clifton Hotel graced this site until it burned in 1932.

To the north of the Falls along the Niagara River Parkway are the Niagara Parks Botanical Gardens and School of Horticulture. Gardening enthusiasts may stroll about the well maintained botanical collections and outstanding landscapes. Adjoining the site and planted in Canada's centennial year, 1967, the Centennial Lilac Garden is a burst of color in May with a profusion of lilacs in hundreds of varieties.

The Niagara Parks Greenhouse just above the Horseshoe Falls is the site of dazzling floral displays. Visitors enjoy colorful seasonal massed floral arrangements and the free flying birds that live in the greenhouse. The Wintergarden is a seven-storey glass enclosed tropical park near the American entrance to the Rainbow Bridge. Both greenhouses may be enjoyed year-round.

On the Niagara Reservation, Goat Island has long been enjoyed for its unspoiled natural beauty and woodland trails. Prospect Park is a well maintained recreational area with enchanting gardens and breathtaking vistas of the Falls.

The Floral Clock is a unique display of 24,000 plants

Stone monument at the entrance to Queen Victoria Park

In the gardens of Prospect Park

In Oakes Garden Theatre

Spectacular floral displays are a hallmark of the Niagara Parks Botanical Gardens

Niagara Parks Commission lands stretch along the entire 56 kilometer (35 mile) west bank of the Niagara River from Lake Erie to Lake Ontario. Winston Churchill described a ride along the Niagara Parkway as "the prettiest Sunday afternoon drive in the world." For those who wish to enjoy the picturesque route at a leisurely pace, a paved path runs alongside the river. The Niagara River Recreation Trail is ideal for bicycling, walking, or roller blading with a splendid view of the Niagara River on one side, and stately historic homes, picnic spots, fruit stands and other points of interest on the other. Golf courses and fishing spots are popular features.

Not all of the Niagara Parks lands are manicured gardens of vivid color. Dufferin Islands is a tranquil natural refuge just above the Horseshoe Falls. Its quiet fishing ponds, winding trails and luxurious greenery make it a popular picnic spot. Some areas of the parkway along the river exhibit natural fauna such as the mounds of prairie grasses indigent to Niagara.

The family vacation estate built by Sir Harry Oakes, on the escarpment above the upper rapids, is now the site of the Niagara Parks Commission administrative offices and a golf course.

An interesting feature in Queen Victoria Park is the Rainbow Tower Carillon. Fifty-five tuned bells, cast in England in the 1940s, serenade visitors to the park. An inscription above the rim of the largest bell, known as the Bourdon, reads "To God's glory and in grateful memory of our nation's leaders, Winston Spencer Churchill and Franklin Delano Roosevelt." An embarrassing controversy occurred over the omission of the name of then Canadian Prime Minister Mackenzie King, but the inscribed dedication remains in place.

A shady resting spot on the Niagara River Recreation Trail

The Recreation Trail follows the west bank of the Niagara River

Golfers enjoy Niagara Parks courses

Oak Hall, home of Niagara Parks offices and a golf course

Dufferin Islands is a tranquil natural refuge

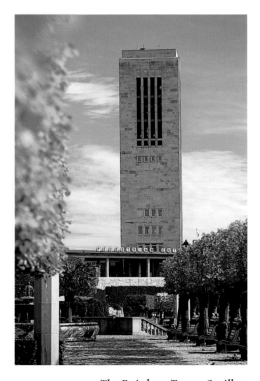

The Rainbow Tower Carillon

As it descends from its headwaters on Lake Erie to the remarkably swift flowing current above the Falls, the Niagara River broadens and narrows, making room for several islands on its way.

Grand Island, the largest of nineteen islands in the upper Niagara River, separates the waters into two channels that reunite for the plunge over the Falls. Densely wooded, the island was a valued hunting and fishing ground for its native inhabitants. In the 1800s, lumbering for wooden barrel staves and clipper ships gave way to ranches, orchards and resort hotels. Grand Island became a popular leisure area with exclusive clubs and elaborate summer homes. Numerous steamers circled the island, ferrying summer vacationers to and from the mainland. Legend has it that the steamboat Huntress was moored near Beaver Island during Prohibition with the International Boundary passing through it amidships, allowing patrons to stiffen their refreshments at the Canadian end of the vessel. Although agitation for a bridge to replace the ferries began as early as 1872, no bridge linked the island to the mainland until 1935. Today Grand Island is a residential area with small boat harbors and scenic parks.

Navy Island, the largest island in Canadian territory, owes its name to the British shipyard built there in 1761. Vessels constructed at the yard navigated the Upper Great Lakes in the days before the Welland Canal. In the late 19th century, a hotel on the east side of Navy Island faced a curving shoreline road used for horse races. Today the island is uninhabited except by herds of deer and other wildlife.

Three Sisters, Luna and several other small islands surround Goat Island near the crest of the Falls. They provide a spectacular view of the upper rapids and neighboring scenery.

A boat house on Grand Island, ca. 1870

Bridge to the Third Sister Island, ca. 1898

A view of the upper rapids from the Third Sister Island

The west bank of the Niagara River, opposite Grand Island

The Treaty of Paris in 1783 set the Niagara River as the International Boundary between British and American territory. The British had established control of the west bank at the river's inlet by building Fort Erie in 1764 on the site of an earlier French trading post. In the years following the American Revolution, British Loyalists left the United States to settle in Canada and a stretch of wilderness along the west bank of the upper Niagara River from the Falls to Fort Erie was reserved for military and defensive purposes. This expanse of land is now a scenic riverside drive.

The frontier became a battleground during the War of 1812. Fort Erie was surrendered to American forces after a fierce battle in 1814. The fort was later destroyed by the Americans, and lay in ruins until it was restored in the 1930s. Now called Historic Fort Erie, it is the site of military reenactments and programs depicting early fort life.

Canadians and Americans are good neighbors today, frequently crossing the Peace Bridge between the Town of Fort Erie and the City of Buffalo. Trade and industry flourished in Buffalo when it became a railway terminus and end point of the Erie Canal in the early 19th century. Today, Buffalo is the second largest city in New York State, surpassed only by New York City.

Canada and the United States work together on the upper Niagara River to battle the effects of winter freeze. Chunks of ice breaking away from the ice cover on Lake Erie and moving downstream towards the Falls have resulted in flooding, serious damage to shore buildings and costly reductions in hydroelectric power generation. To minimize these effects, Ontario Hydro and New York Power Authority icebreakers patrol the river, crushing the frozen masses, and an ice boom is installed each year in Lake Erie. The boom extends from the outer breakwater at Buffalo harbor almost to the Canadian shore.

Icebreakers on the upper Niagara River

An ice boom reduces the severity of ice runs in the Niagara River

On guard at Historic Fort Erie

Historic Fort Erie was built in 1764

Buffalo dominates the headwaters of the Niagara River at Lake Erie

A view of Buffalo from Fort Erie

The Niagara River below the Falls rushes headlong through a deep and narrow gorge to the great Whirlpool. As the water escapes the swirling vortex, it takes a right-angled turn and charges furiously on its course towards a point, at Lewiston and Queenston, where the surrounding land drops abruptly. This ridge, known as the Niagara escarpment, runs roughly parallel to Lake Ontario's shore. From the escarpment, a quieter course begins as the river broadens and flows majestically into Lake Ontario.

The Whirlpool is the natural result of a mighty torrent of water rushing into a confined space and seeking an outlet. Everything that goes over the Falls finds its way into the Whirlpool, where it may circle for some time before being thrown out onto the bank or it may be carried on down the river towards Lake Ontario. When the water level is low because of diversion for power generation, the river moves clockwise through the Whirlpool to the natural outlet. A reversal phenomenon occurs, however, when the Niagara River is at full flow. The water travels counterclockwise around the basin, passing the outlet. Pressure builds as the water tries to cut across itself to reach the outlet; the pressure forces the water beneath the incoming stream.

The Whirlpool Rapids rival the awesome beauty and drama of the Falls themselves. Approaching the Whirlpool, the river leaps and thunders through the narrow canyon carved by the receding Falls over thousands of years.

Another set of rapids roars through the gorge below the Whirlpool. This is the narrowest stretch of the Niagara River. An American company once planned to take advantage of this proximity by building an arch bridge across the canyon at this point. The bridge bill passed the New York State Assembly but failed in the Senate, because there were fears that rattlesnakes would cross the bridge and infest the United States. At that time, timber rattlesnakes were among the natural wonders of the Niagara Glen on the Canadian bank.

The lower Niagara River rushes into the Whirlpool

A jet ski rider challenges the treacherous rapids of the Niagara River below the Whirlpool

Lower Niagara River

For the adventurous, various hiking trails lead down the steep walled gorge of the lower Niagara River to the water's edge. Those who make the descent are rewarded with an unparalleled view of the rapids and the thundering roar of their fury.

A popular hiking trail on the American bank follows the path taken by the Great Gorge Route streetcars a century ago. Along this path, at Devil's Hole, the river reaches its narrowest point. Close to the water, a wedge shaped limestone rock about two storeys high is one of many pieces of rock that avalanched down as the Falls retreated and carved out the gorge many centuries ago.

On the Canadian shore, the Niagara Glen nature reserve is a wonderland for botanists, geologists, and naturalists. Spectacular rock formations dot the woodland trails. A mammoth pothole in a limestone boulder is just one of many wonders giving evidence of the turbulent, erosive force of the Niagara River that charged through this area more than 9000 years ago.

Hikers have enjoyed the incomparable natural beauty of the Glen for more than a century. When accompanying the Prince of Wales to Niagara Falls in 1860, Nicholas Woods remarked, "if the Falls were not there, the exquisite combination of rock and woodland all around would suffice to draw visitors from all parts of North America."

Fishing enthusiasts find that gorge conditions make it the perfect habitat for rainbow trout, chinook salmon, smallmouth bass and other desirable coldwater species. It is the also the home of numerous species of herons, ducks and gulls. In fact, the Niagara River corridor is a birding area of global renown, with the largest and most diverse concentration of gulls in the world.

A mammoth pothole in the Niagara Glen

Recreational fishing is a popular activity in the Niagara Gorge

The Niagara River is a renowned birding corridor

In the Niagara Glen, ca. 1906

A giant rock on the American bank

Lower Niagara River

The high banks of the lower Niagara River afford a panoramic view of its winding course. The river broadens as it flows serenely northward from the villages of Queenston and Lewiston. Both communities were thriving ports on the portage routes around the Falls in the 18th and early 19th centuries. On opposite banks as the river flows into Lake Ontario are the historic towns of Niagara-on-the-Lake, the first capital of Upper Canada, and Youngstown, New York.

Military forts sprang up on both sides of the Niagara River in the 18th century. Their prominence as supply and shipment points was equal to their role in stabilizing the vast and newly acquired territories to the west. Built by the French in the 1720s, Old Fort Niagara at Youngstown, New York, commands the mouth of the Niagara River at Lake Ontario. It was taken by the British in 1759 but relinquished to American troops in 1796 under the terms of the Jay Treaty. The British garrison subsequently moved into newly built Fort George on the Canadian shore.

The garrisons sprang into action when war broke out along the border in 1812. British and Canadian forces won a fierce battle against invading American troops at Queenston Heights. American artillery at Fort Niagara bombarded and destroyed Fort George. It was reconstructed in the 1930s to appear as it did before 1813.

Visitors now enjoy military reenactments and historic tent camps at Fort George and Old Fort Niagara. Original stone buildings at Old Fort Niagara are the oldest in the Great Lakes region.

A view of the lower Niagara River and distant Lewiston-Queenston bridge

A green heron wades the shoreline in Niagara-on-the-Lake

Fort George was British headquarters from 1796 until 1813

Old Fort Niagara dominates the mouth of the Niagara River at Lake Ontario

Visitors enjoy a military reenactment at Fort George

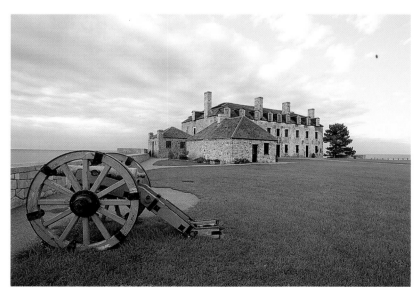

In the 1700s, Old Fort Niagara flew the French, British and American flags

The Maid of the Mist

The Maid of the Mist tour boats are known all over the world. They provide a ride right into the mist of Niagara Falls.

The first Maid of the Mist navigated the waters below the Falls as a ferry service, not a sightseeing boat. A side-wheeler steamboat with twin smokestacks, it was built at the American landing in 1846 and launched amid cheering crowds, band music and joyful toasts to its success. The days of crossing the river below the Falls in tiny rowboats were near an end. With no bridge yet spanning the Niagara Gorge, entrepreneurs with rowboats had been ferrying passengers across the gorge since 1818. A trip between the American and Canadian landings in one of the tiny rowboats took about eight minutes. In the interest of improving this service to accommodate mail, freight and tourists with baggage, the Maid of the Mist trips began.

Within a few years of the first Maid's launch, the first suspension bridge spanned the Niagara Gorge and the ferry business declined. The owners of the Maid of the Mist recognized a new opportunity and began sightseeing trips close to the Falls that continue today.

A 1905 advertisement promoted "a Novel, Exciting and Charming Steamboat Trip. Staunch and powerful steamers carry the tourist up to the foot of the American and Horseshoe Falls in the great gorge of the Niagara. Fare (including rubber clothing furnished on the boat) Fifty Cents."

A description in the *Niagara Courier* of the launch of the first Maid of the Mist in 1846 seems as apt today as it was then: "the scenery around, the majesty of the thundering cataract above, the fierce rapids, the high embankment on both sides...combine to produce a scene surpassingly good and romantic. Whoever visits Niagara will not have seen half its wonders till they have taken a trip on the Maid."

The Maid of the Mist passes the American and Bridal Veil Falls

The Maid of the Mist approaches the Horseshoe Falls

The Maid of the Mist

For more than 150 years, Maid of the Mist vessels have operated from the American and Canadian landings, taking passengers past the American and Bridal Veil Falls into the pool below the Horseshoe Falls.

Eleven different Maids have plied the waters of the Niagara Gorge below the Falls. A Maid of the Mist advertisement in 1854 proclaimed that a new single stack paddle wheel steamer had been built without regard to expense, and furnished with lifeboats and all the modern improvements. "She is 170 tons burden, propelled by a powerful engine of 100 horsepower, built expressly for this route." Improvements over the years have enhanced the size and performance of each new vessel. When the Maid of the Mist VII was launched in 1997, it boasted twin 350 horsepower diesel engines and a capacity of 600 passengers.

Maid of the Mist boats in their winter berths on the Canadian shore were threatened by great ice jams below the Falls in 1938 and again in 1997. The ice that toppled the Honeymoon Bridge in 1938 rose nearly level with their decks. In the spring of 1997, two Maids were floated off their cradles and encased in ice and debris.

Two early Maid of the Mist steamboats, built in 1885 and 1892, provided many decades of reliable service. They survived the ice jam of 1938 but were destroyed by fire in April 1955. A welder's torch set the wooden boats ablaze shortly before the spring launch. They were replaced by new vessels made entirely of steel.

The Canadian docks, 1996, celebrating the Maid's 150th year

A 1907 postcard shows a steam powered Maid of the Mist

Maid of the Mist V passes beneath the Horseshoe Falls near Terrapin Point

Journey Behind the Falls

When the "Great New Scenic Tunnel" opened at Table Rock, an advertising pamphlet extolled the wonders of the attraction. "Now Open! See the marvelous and ever changing sights behind the great Horseshoe Fall. The constant spray and mist form fancy icicles any time with temperatures at freezing point."

An 1833 guidebook promoted the "convenient passage" to the "celebrated spot" behind the Falls. As one traveler reported, it was decidedly perilous, but it was "the thing" to do to be fashionable. Thousands of visitors donned raincoats at Table Rock House and descended a circular stairway to reach the base of the Falls. A crude wooden walkway wound around fallen rocks and afforded a breathtaking view. By 1887, a hydraulic lift was installed and a tunnel was cut through the rock behind the Falls a few years later. Guides carried lanterns and led visitors through the tunnel passage. As the brink of the Horseshoe Falls receded over the years, it was necessary to extend or reroute the old tunnel. By the end of World War II, the walls of the main tunnel were perilously close to the edge of the waterfall and a new tunnel was cut much deeper into the rock.

Still open year-round, the attraction is now known as the Journey Behind the Falls. An outdoor observation deck provides an astonishing view of the mighty torrent of water rushing over the Horseshoe Falls. Other tunnels lead to openings cut in the rock behind the raging waterfall.

From the vantage point of the tunnel openings, the sound is extraordinary. In 1935, a microphone was placed at the end of the deepest tunnel in order to broadcast the roar of Niagara Falls to listeners worldwide.

Visitors to the Journey Behind the Falls emerge from tunnels beneath Table Rock

Sightseers view the mighty Horseshoe Falls at close range

The view from the tunnels has thrilled tourists for more than a century

"Below the Falls in Winter, Table Rock Tunnel," ca. 1890

Cave of the Winds

An elevator on Goat Island descends to the Cave of the Winds at the base of the Bridal Veil Falls in the Niagara Gorge. A series of wooden walkways and the aptly named Hurricane Deck give visitors a spectacular view of the Falls.

More than a century ago, visitors hiked down a stairway to river level amid massive fallen boulders that once formed the floor of the upper rapids. Struggling against torrents of spray and wind, they ventured into a natural cavern in the face of the gorge behind the Bridal Veil Falls. This cave collapsed in 1920, preventing further access to it.

The Cave of the Winds experience is perhaps best described by the American writer, Mark Twain, who wrote of his descent in 1869 "below the precipice, down a winding flight of stairs...along flimsy bridges"...and slashed by a "furious wind that seemed determined to sweep us from the bridge and scatter us on the rocks and among the torrents below....We were almost under the monstrous wall of water thundering down from above and speech was in vain in the midst of such a pitiless crash of sound....bewildered by the thunder, driven helplessly by the wind and smitten by the arrowy tempest of rain....I bent my head, and seemed to receive the Atlantic on my back...I raised my head, with open mouth, and the most of the American cataract went down my throat. If I had sprung a leak now I had been lost...I never was so scared before and survived it."

The walkways of the Cave of the Winds in the Niagara Gorge

The plunging torrent of the Bridal Veil Falls descends towards the walkways of the Cave of the Winds

As the Niagara River winds downstream from the Falls, the gorge narrows and the current races swiftly through the canyon, thundering into the giant Whirlpool. Visitors can get an unsurpassed view of the spectacle from the edge of the Niagara River or from above.

Great Gorge Adventure

An elevator descends to the base of the gorge and opens onto a wooden boardwalk along the edge of the rapids. Experiencing the awesome roar of the white water is as thrilling to many visitors as seeing the stupendous power of the turbulent river at close range.

Niagara Spanish Aero Car

High above the raging Niagara River, the Aero Car crosses to and fro, carrying sightseers over the Whirlpool. At this point, the tumultuous rapids swirl into the giant vortex and then turn abruptly northeast to escape into the narrowest channel in the gorge.

A favorite with visitors from all over the world, the Aero Car was named for the Spanish engineer, Leonardo Torres-Quevedo, who designed and built it in 1916. The operating machinery was set right into the gorge wall at the Colt's Point ticket station and at the opposite landing platform at Thompson Point. Tourists were at first reluctant to trust the safety of the new and daring ride, but the Niagara Spanish Aero Car proved to be a secure means of transportation, with its sturdy cables in use for 35 years before they needed to be replaced. In recent years, the entire cable car system has been renovated and upgraded to ensure continued safety.

View of the Niagara River from the boardwalk of the Great Gorge Adventure

The Aero Car began operating in 1916

The Niagara Spanish Aero Car crosses the Niagara Gorge above its swirling Whirlpool

Whirlpool Jet Boats

Those with a sense of adventure can challenge the rapids of the Niagara River gorge aboard a Whirlpool Jet Boat. This ride is not for the fainthearted!

Jet boats departing from Niagara-on-the-Lake, Ontario, and Lewiston, New York, travel upriver through the Niagara River canyon towards the Whirlpool. Each boat is equipped with three diesel engines totalling 1600 horsepower. Passing the turbulent Class 3 rapids just beyond the Robert Moses and Sir Adam Beck power stations, the jet boat moves into Class 5 waves at Devil's Hole, just below the Whirlpool. Class 5 rapids such as these must be navigated with extreme caution. No river ride in North America attempts any higher class of rapids.

The jet boats do not enter the Class 6 rapids above the Whirlpool. These rapids are the fiercest in North America and are not considered navigable. Riverman Ken Sloggett, who has been involved in many rescues and is considered an expert on the Niagara River, describes this stretch of water as too unpredictable for navigation. The rapids above the Whirlpool, he says, "are the type that make the hair on the back of your neck stand up." Some eddies are like a bathtub when it is draining out, pulling everything under as the water swirls around. Attempts in the 1970s to provide rides for tourists through these Class 6 rapids above the Whirlpool proved disastrous.

The calm before the storm

A jet boat challenges the turbulent Niagara River rapids

Passengers in rain suits are soaked with spray and immersed in river water

Brock's Monument

Queenston Park is a popular stop on the scenic drive along the west bank of the lower Niagara River. Towering above the Niagara escarpment on Queenston Heights is Brock's Monument, a symbol of Loyalist supremacy. It is a tribute to the legendary hero, Major-General Sir Isaac Brock, the commander of British forces who lost his life in a clash with American troops during the War of 1812. Brock is credited with saving Canada from American rule by gallantly storming the heights at Queenston and urging his men on with the words, "Push on, brave York Volunteers."

The Butterfly Conservatory

When the Niagara Parks Butterfly Conservatory opened to the public in 1996, it was an immediate sensation. The world's largest glass enclosed butterfly conservatory became a very popular attraction for visitors to Niagara Falls.

Located north of the Falls on the grounds of the Niagara Parks Botanical Gardens and School of Horticulture, the conservatory is a climate controlled paradise of exotic foliage, flowing water and colorful blooms. Visitors may walk a network of pathways amid the fluttering and darting flight of hundreds of the delicate creatures. Butterflies of all hues may be spotted on the tropical plants on which they feed, and even on the clothing of visitors to the exhibit. More than 2000 butterflies of 50 different species can be observed at close range.

A hatching area provides a look at the four stages in the life cycle of the butterfly. Many of the butterflies on display are raised in the hatchery; others are imported from butterfly farms around the world.

Brock's Monument in Queenston Park

At the Butterfly Conservatory

Visitors get a closeup view

A Julia draws nectar from the Mexican Flame Vine

An aerial view of the greenhouses and conservatory

The Schoellkopf Geological Museum

A multiscreen presentation, museum exhibits, a geological garden and naturalist-led tours into the precipitous Niagara Gorge provide visitors with an appreciation of how the Falls took shape over time and how they influenced the human history of the area. The Schoellkopf Geological Museum overlooks the Niagara River in the state parkland just north of the American Falls.

Benjamin Franklin, the famous American scientist and statesman, wrote to the editor of a London newspaper in 1765 that "the grand leap of the whale up the Fall of Niagara is esteemed, by all who have seen it, as one of the finest spectacles in nature." Although he was teasing the British for their ignorance of America, and there are, indeed, no whales in the Niagara River, it is ironic that the mighty whale and other sea animals are now popular features at two Niagara attractions.

The Aquarium

The Aquarium in Niagara Falls, New York, is home to 1500 aquatic animals, including sharks, piranhas, penguins and sea lions, and the largest collection of Great Lakes fishes anywhere. Displays and educational programs are open year-round.

Marineland

Marineland in Niagara Falls, Ontario, is a theme park with marine shows, amusement rides and wildlife displays. At outdoor and indoor theaters, visitors enjoy the antics of killer whales, sea lions and dolphins. A walk through the park provides encounters at close range with Canadian elk, deer, buffalo and bear.

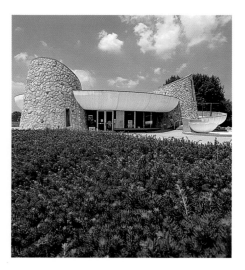

The Schoellkopf Geological Museum

The Aquarium of Niagara

Visitors can walk among herds of deer at Marineland

The majestic killer whale can be friendly and playful

A killer whale is magnificent at close range

The Niagara area hosts a variety of attractions a short distance from the Falls.

Artpark sits on the heights above the Niagara River in Lewiston, New York. It features performances throughout the summer season ranging from jazz and popular music to ballet and musical theater. Unique daytime arts programs and workshops are enjoyed by all ages.

Niagara-on-the-Lake, the first capital of Upper Canada, is the home of the Shaw Festival, celebrating the works of George Bernard Shaw and his contemporaries. Victorian, Edwardian and Georgian plays are presented at three theaters in the historic town. A miniature Wayside Chapel along the winding Niagara River Parkway is a popular stop on the route north of the Falls, approaching Niagara-on-the-Lake.

The Niagara Region Wine Route meanders through some beautiful rural Ontario landscape. The rich soils of the area are well suited to the harvesting of premium grapes. Long before the earliest settler arrived, grapes were growing wild in Canada and there are records of Canadian wines being produced by Jesuit priests as early as 1636. Several wineries were operating in Niagara by 1881 and the area's wines now win international acclaim. Niagara wines are available for tasting at many wineries along the route which offer tours, special events and wine sampling. The ice wines of Niagara enjoy worldwide renown.

West of Niagara Falls and running parallel to the Niagara River, the Welland Canal is a pathway for vessels climbing around Niagara Falls. Shippers of iron ore, grain and manufactured goods have long appreciated this route between the upper Great Lakes and the Saint Lawrence River to and from the Atlantic Ocean. Oceangoing ships were never able to navigate the shallow channels of the Erie Canal through New York State or its successor, the Barge Canal, so the Welland Canal, built in 1829 and updated several times, became one of the busiest and most important waterways in the world.

Artpark is situated on the bluffs at Lewiston, New York

Niagara-on-the-Lake is home of the Shaw Festival Theater

A miniature chapel on the Niagara River Parkway welcomes visitors

Niagara wineries offer tours and wine tasting

The Welland Canal was built in 1829 to bypass the Falls

More and more tourists are enjoying a magnificent view of the Falls from the air. Helicopter tours are available from both sides of the border, providing a unique look at the Whirlpool and rapids of the Niagara Gorge, the American and Horseshoe Falls and surrounding parklands. At ground level, narrated tours are available in Canada on an authentic double deck bus from London, England. The bus stops at the Falls and popular attractions.

Observation towers have been popular with tourists for more than a hundred years. Modern towers with swift elevators have replaced the early towers with their winding stairways. The Terrapin Tower at the American side of the Horseshoe Falls, a landmark from 1833 to 1873, was built of fieldstones gathered in the area. Street's Pagoda, built in 1860, was a wooden structure on Cedar Island just above the Falls. Today, the New York State Observation Tower on the American bank and the Skylon Tower on the opposite shore stand high above the surrounding landscape at the Falls.

The former Maple Leaf Village Tower in Niagara Falls, Ontario, is the site of Casino Niagara, a world class casino that is the largest in Canada. Just walking distance from the Falls, Casino Niagara is a gaming, dining and entertainment complex that is open around the clock every day of the year.

Helicopter tours provide a breathtaking view of the Falls from the air

Narrated tours can be taken aboard a double deck bus

Casino Niagara opened in 1996

Casino Niagara is an opulent setting for gaming, dining and entertainment

The Skylon Tower is one of several observation towers for viewing the Falls

Niagara Falls by night has a special beauty all its own. Moonlight playing upon the tumbling waters has a mystical quality that has been a favorite subject of landscape painters. Today, twinkling lights and colored spotlights create a sense of magic in the gardens surrounding the Falls. Even more dramatic is the spectacle created by colored lights that shine upon the thundering waters of the American and Horseshoe Falls every evening. One visitor described the sight this way: "To see the Falls at night is to be wide awake in the land of dreams."

The Falls were lit up for the first time in 1860, the night before Blondin crossed the Niagara Gorge on a tightrope to entertain Albert Edward, Prince of Wales, who later became King Edward VII. At that time, 200 lights were placed along the banks above the Falls, all about on the rocks below, and on the road leading down the Canadian bank. Called "Bengal" lights, the colored and white, calcium, volcanic and torpedo lights were set aflame all at once. *The London Times* reported that the Prince of Wales saw the cataracts as "no man had seen them before...illuminated first in silver, like cascades of diamonds, then in red like blood, then blue."

Electricity helped light up the Falls in later years, but it was not until 1925 that 24 carbon arc searchlights began illuminating both Falls, with color screens for each projector creating a vast array of color combinations. Today, powerful searchlights continue to shine on the Falls at night. Rich hues are projected across the gorge from the roof of the Ontario Hydro surge tank in Queen Victoria Park, creating a glorious rainbow or a mass of brilliant color.

Niagara is a rainbow of color at night

Searchlights beam from the Ontario Hydro surge tank in Queen Victoria Park

Bright lights illuminate the Falls at night year-round

Winter Festival of Lights

Colored lights twinkle from trees, towers and land-marks near the Falls during the annual international Winter Festival of Lights. Lighting displays the length of Queen Victoria Park excite the imagination. In Niagara Falls, New York, decorated pedestrian walkways, animated displays and the world's largest light-sound synthesizer contribute to the international celebration. Special events and outdoor concerts on a stage near the Falls turn winter evenings into a magical time in a breathtaking setting.

Clifton Hill

A profusion of sights and sounds greets curiosity seekers on Clifton Hill and adjoining streets in Niagara Falls, Canada. Dozens of museums, shops, restaurants and amusements cater to tastes from the historical to the garish. Flashing neon lights and music draw attention to everything from sweets to wax figures of the famous.

Fireworks

Regular fireworks displays over the Falls are a sight not to be missed. Thunderous booms resonate from the gorge walls as showers of color burst over the rushing water. The fireworks are a marvelous spectacle from vantage points in the parkland by the Falls or from hotels and observation towers nearby.

The Winter Festival of Lights is an international celebration

Bright lights and excitement abound at Clifton Hill

A burst of fireworks illuminates the Falls

Michael D. Romanowich

This book features the exceptional photographic work of Michael D. Romanowich, a native of Niagara. He now resides in Waterloo, Ontario. His photographs also appear in *Historic Niagara-on- the-Lake, A Pictorial Discovery*, 1995.

Bill and Margaret Dunn

Niagara Falls, A Pictorial Journey is the second book by Margaret Dunn. A free-lance writer and publisher, she is the author of *Historic Niagara-on-the-Lake, A Pictorial Discovery*, 1995. Her husband, Bill Dunn, played an integral part in the promotion, photo selection, and historic works reproduction for this book. Bill and Margaret Dunn are residents of Niagara Falls, Canada.

Pictorial Credits

The excellent contemporary photographs by Michael D. Romanowich, more than 90 in total, are supplemented by the following historical works and images:

Inside cover   Scugog Shores Historical Museum

Page 2   *The Great Horseshoe – Niagara.* Paul Thomas Hanover. Oil, 1991. Rolling Thunder Arts, Inc.

NATURAL WONDER
Page 12   Lower: Author's Collection

TWO NATIONS IN HARMONY
Page 20   Lower: Author's Collection

FROM WILDERNESS TO WORLDWIDE FAME
Pages 22-23   *Father Hennepin at Niagara Falls*, Thomas Hart Benton. New York Power Authority.

Page 24   Upper: Reproduction of *The Falls of Niagara*, unidentified artist, engraving in Louis Hennepin: "Nouvelle Decouverte d'un Tres Grand Pays Situe dans l'Amerique," Utrecht, 1697. Niagara Falls Public Library (ON), City of Niagara Falls Collection.
Lower: *Falls of Niagara*, Isaac Weld (attrib.), 1796. The Weir Foundation, Queenston, Ontario.

Page 25   *Niagara Falls from the Canadian Side*, Hippolyte Sebron, ca. 1850. The Weir Foundation, Queenston, Ontario.

Page 26   Upper: *The "43rd Light Infantry" as They "Turn Out" in their Sleighs at the "Falls of Niagara,"* Sir Richard George Augustus Levinge, 1839. Metropolitan Toronto Reference Library, J. Ross Robertson Collection MTL2164
Lower: *The Falls of Niagara: This View of the HorseShoe Fall from Goat Island*, James Pattison Cockburn, 1833. Private Collection.

Page 27   *Niagara*, Frederic E. Church, 1857. Oil on canvas in the Collection of the Corcoran Gallery of Art, Washington, DC.

Page 28   Upper: Paul Thomas Hanover Collection.
Lower: Reproduction of *Table Rock*, ca. 1846, from "Niagara Falls and Scenes Around Them," J. W. Ferree, 1876, British Museum, London. Niagara Falls Public Library (ON), Niagara Falls Heritage Foundation Collection.

Page 29   All: Niagara Falls Public Library (NY).

Page 30   Upper and lower: Niagara Falls Public Library (NY).

Page 31   *Terrapin Tower – Niagara*, Paul Thomas Hanover. Oil, 1997. Rolling Thunder Arts Inc.

Page 32   Upper: Reproduction of an 1847 sketch (anonymous); watercolor by Donna Campbell. Niagara Falls Public Library (ON), City of Niagara Falls Collection.
Lower: Reproduction of *The Niagara Falls Suspension Bridge, first Opened August 1, 1848*, lithograph by Wm. Endicott and Co. Niagara Falls Public Library (ON), Chamber of Commerce Collection.

Page 33   Reproduction of *Railway Suspension Bridge*, from "Niagara Falls and Scenes Around Them" by J. W. Ferree, 1876, British Museum, London. Niagara Falls Public Library (ON), Niagara Falls Heritage Foundation Collection.

Page 34   Upper and lower: Antique postcards, Author's Collection.

Page 35   *View of Canada Southern Train Passing Niagara Falls*, artist unknown, ca. 1880. The Weir Foundation, Queenston, Ontario.

Page 36   Upper and lower: Francis Petrie Collection.

Page 37   Scugog Shores Historical Museum.

Page 38   Upper: Robert Bracken Collection.
Lower: City of Toronto Archives' Globe & Mail Collection SC266-86631.

Page 39   Left: Ron Schifferle.
Upper right: Fred Green Collection.
Lower right: Clarence Joyce Collection.

Page 40   Upper: Ron Roels.
Lower: Maid of the Mist Steamboat Company, Ltd.

Page 41   George Bailey.

DAREDEVILS
Page 42   Len Rosenberg, Rochester Collection.

Page 43   All: Niagara Falls Public Library (NY).

Page 44   Upper left: Niagara Falls Public Library (ON).
Upper right: Niagara Falls Public Library (NY).
Lower: Lou Riccuiti, Henry Andrews.

Page 45   Left: Pat Simon Collection.
Upper and lower right: Niagara Falls Public Library (NY).

Page 46   Upper: Author's Collection.

Page 47   Left: Author's Collection.
Right: Niagara Falls Public Library (NY).

Page 48   Lundy's Lane Historical Museum.

Page 49   Niagara Falls Public Library (NY).

Page 50   Upper: Antique postcard, Author's Collection.
Lower: Francis Petrie Collection.

Page 51   Left: Niagara Falls Public Library (NY).
Upper and lower right: Ron Roels.

Page 52   Upper: Antique postcard, Sherman Zavitz Collection.
Lower: Author's Collection.

Page 53   All: Ron Roels.

Page 54   Upper and lower: Niagara Falls Public Library (NY).

Page 55   Left: Don Ede.
Right: Michael Bailey.

HEADLINE NEWS EVENTS
Page 56   Upper: Ron Schifferle.
Lower: Niagara Falls Public Library (NY).

Page 57   Left: Niagara Falls Public Library (ON).
Upper right: Fred Green Collection.
Lower right: Clarence Joyce Collection.

Page 58   Francis Petrie Collection.

Page 59   Upper and lower left: Francis Petrie Collection.
Right: Niagara Falls Public Library (ON).

Page 60   Upper: John Burtniak Collection.

Page 61   J. Stuart Fleming Collection.

Pages 62-63   Francis Petrie Collection.

THE FALLS IN WINTER
Pages 64-65   Bill Dunn.

Page 66   Antique postcards, Author's Collection.

Page 67   Left: Antique postcards, Author's Collection.
Right: *Coasting below the American Falls*, 1880. Lundy's Lane Historical Museum.

Page 68   Upper: Niagara Falls Public Library (NY).
Lower: Pat Simon Collection.

Page 69   Antique postcards, Author's Collection.

NIAGARA FOLKLORE
Page 71   Left: *The Red Man's Fact: The Maiden Sacrifice*, James Francis Brown, 1891. Buffalo and Erie County Historical Society.
Right: *The White Man's Fancy: The Maid of the Mist*, James Francis Brown, 1891. Buffalo and Erie County Historical Society.

Page 72   *The Hermit of Niagara*, Laurel Campbell. Watercolor, 1997. Author's Collection.

Page 73   Reproduction of *American Fall from Goat Island*, W. J. Bennett, ca. 1830, National Archives of Canada. Niagara Falls Public Library (ON), Niagara Falls Heritage Foundation Collection.

POWER
Page 74   Upper: Antique postcard, Author's Collection.

Page 75   *Six Million Wild Horses*, artist unknown, ca. 1924. Niagara Mohawk Power Corporation.

Page 77   Bill Dunn.

Page 78   Upper: Niagara Falls Public Library (ON).

Page 83   Left: Bill Dunn.

PARKS AND GARDENS
Page 87   Lower left: Bobb Barratt.

THE UPPER NIAGARA RIVER
Page 91   Upper left: Author's Collection.
Right: Ron Paré.

Page 92   Both: New York Power Authority.

Page 93   Upper right and lower left: Bill Dunn.

THE LOWER NIAGARA RIVER
Page 96   Upper: Bill Dunn.

Page 97   Upper right: Antique postcard, Author's Collection.

ATTRACTIONS
Page 102   Lower: Antique postcard, Author's Collection.

Page 105   Lower right: Antique postcard, Author's Collection.

Page 109   Right: Francis Petrie Collection.

Page 112   Bill Dunn.

Page 113   Lower right: Bill Dunn.

Page 116   Upper: Bill Dunn.

Page 117   Right: Bill Dunn.

Page 122   Upper: A Festival of Lights, Niagara Falls, NY/Jim McCoy.

Page 124   Lower: Bob Harasty.

Every reasonable effort has been made to contact all of the sources and copyright holders of the materials cited. The author regrets any oversight or omission.

Bibliography

Adamson, Jeremy E. *Niagara: Two Centuries of Changing Attitudes, 1697-1901.* Washington: Corcoran Gallery of Art, 1985.

Aug, Lisa. *Beyond the Falls: A Modern History of the Lower Niagara River.* Niagara Falls, NY: Niagara Books, 1992.

Bailey, George. *The Magic of Niagara.* Toronto: Royal Specialty Sales, 1996.

Berton, Pierre. *Niagara.* Toronto: McClelland & Stewart, 1992.

Braider, Donald. *The Niagara.* New York: Holt, Rinehart and Winston, 1972.

Buffalo Fine Arts Academy. *Three Centuries of Niagara Falls.* Buffalo: Albright-Knox Art Gallery, 1964.

Dow, Charles M. *Anthology and Bibliography of Niagara Falls, Vol. I and II.* Albany: State of New York, 1921.

Dumych, Daniel M. *Niagara Falls.* Dover, NH: Arcadia Publishing, 1996.

Granfield, Linda. *All About Niagara Falls.* Toronto: Kids Can Press, 1988.

Greenhill, Ralph, and Mahoney, Thomas D. *Niagara.* Toronto: University of Toronto Press, 1969.

Holder, Thomas. *A Complete Record of Niagara Falls and Vicinage.* Niagara Falls, NY, 1882.

Holley, George W. *The Falls of Niagara.* New York: Armstrong and Son, 1883.

Hulbert, A. B. *The Niagara River.* New York: G. P. Putnam's Sons, 1908.

Impressions of Niagara – Charles Rand Penney Collection. Philadelphia Print Shop, 1993.

MacLeod, Rob Roy. *Cinderella Island.* Grand Island Chamber of Commerce, 1969.

McKinsey, Elizabeth. *Niagara Falls, Icon of the American Sublime.* New York: Cambridge University Press, 1985.

O'Brien, Andy. *Daredevils of Niagara.* Toronto: Ryerson Press, 1964.

Parsons, Horatio. *A Guide to Travelers Visiting the Falls of Niagara.* Buffalo, NY: Oliver G. Steele, 1834.

Parsons, Horatio. *The Book of Niagara Falls.* Buffalo, NY: Oliver G. Steele, 1836.

Petrie, Francis. *Roll Out the Barrel.* Erin, Ontario: The Boston Mills Press, 1985.

Porter, Peter A. *The Niagara Region in History.* New York: Cassier Magazine Co., 1895.

Porter, Peter A. *Goat Island.* Niagara Falls, NY, 1900.

Porter, Peter A. *Official Guide to Niagara Falls, River, Frontier.* Buffalo: Matthews-Northrup Works, 1901.

Seibel, George. *Bridges Over the Niagara Gorge.* Niagara Falls, Ontario: The Niagara Falls Bridge Commission, 1991.

Seibel, George. *Niagara Falls, Canada.* Niagara Falls: Kiwanis Club of Stamford, 1967.

Seibel, George. *Ontario's Niagara Parks, 100 Years.* Niagara Falls, Ontario: The Niagara Parks Commission, 1985.

Seibel, George. *The Niagara Portage Road.* The City of Niagara Falls, Ontario, 1990.

Tammemagi, Hans and Allyson. *Exploring Niagara.* St. Catharines: Oakhill Publishing House, 1997.

Taylor, Annie Edson. *Over the Falls, How the Horseshoe Fall was Conquered.* A. E. Taylor, 1902

The Falls of Niagara. Chicago: Knight, Leonard & Co., 1892.

Tiplin, A. H. *Our Romantic Niagara.* Niagara Falls, Ontario: Niagara Falls Heritage Foundation, 1988.

Vidler, Virginia. *Niagara Falls, One Hundred Years of Souvenirs.* Utica: North Country Books, Inc., 1985.

Vogel, Michael N. *Echoes in the Mist: An Illustrated History of the Niagara Falls Area.* Chatsworth: Windsor Publications, Inc., 1991.

Whalen, Dwight. *Lovers' Guide to Niagara Falls.* Niagara Falls, Ontario: Horseshoe Press, 1990.

Williams, Edward T. *Scenic and Historic Niagara Falls.* Niagara Falls, New York, 1925.

Williams, Marjorie F. *A Brief History of Niagara Falls, New York.* Niagara Falls Public Library, 1972.

Zavitz, Sherman L. *Niagara Then and Now.* Niagara-on-the-Lake: Avenue Park Publishing, 1996.

Zavitz, Sherman L. *It Happened at Niagara, First Series.* Niagara Falls, Ontario: The Lundy's Lane Historical Society, 1996.

Index